HOME AND WORLD: INDIAN DIASPORIC READING

Dr. T. Senthamarai
Associate Professor, Department of English
VELS Institute of Science, Technology and Advanced Studies, Chennai

Dr. M. R. Chandran
Associate Professor and Head, Centre for Research in English,
Saraswathi Narayanan College (Autonomous), Madurai

SHANLAX #SINCE1990
SHANLAX PUBLICATIONS

HOME AND WORLD: INDIAN DIASPORIC READING

First Edition: September 2020

ISBN: 978-93-90082-64-3

Price: ₹ 230/-

Publisher
SHANLAX PUBLICATIONS
61, 66 T.P.K. Main Road
Vasantha Nagar
Madurai – 625003
Tamil Nadu, India

Ph: 0452-4208765,
Mobile: 7639303383
email:publisher@shanlaxpublications.com
web: www.shanlaxpublications.com

Forward.....

Indian Diaspora Literature is the body of literary works by the Indians away from their homeland. The writers nurse their feelings of wanting in being away in a distant land, hence their effort to embrace their native roots. This literature documents diaspora issues like dislocation, fragmentation, nostalgia for home, marginalization, racial hatred, cultural and gender issues, identity crisis, generational conflicts, hybrid pattern of life born out of cross-cultural interaction. However, the writers' concerns differ to a great extent in response to their generation, individual perception and their community. The writers also reflect the attempt of the immigrants to adapt, assimilate and amalgamate with the society of the host country but not drying up their concern to maintain their authentic relationship with native culture and identity. This book attempts to bring out varied notions of diaspora feelings of Indian Writers.

CONTENTS

KETAKI KUSHARI DYSON – A SELF PROCLAIMED DIASPORIC WRITER

Anindita Chatterjee,
Assistant Teacher, Rishra Girls' High School, West Bengal

Ketaki Kushari Dyson, best known for her novel titled "*Rabindranath O Victoria Ocampor Sandhaney*" is a lifelong explorer of new expressions, new way of writing, new knowledge, new language, new civilizations, and cultures. She is a writer of the Bengali diaspora who is read widely in India, Bangladesh and wherever there are diasporic Bengali-speaking communities in the world. Born in 1940 she had her school education and the first phase of university education in Calcutta, India. This extremely bright student of English literature had her Ph.D. from Oxford University. In 1964 she migrated to England after marrying Dr. Robert Dyson, a British physicist. Thereafter she started an altogether new journey of her life. Ketaki is one of those gifted writers who profusely write both in English and Bengali with equal expertise. She has shown mastery in different genres of writing: poetry, fiction, plays, literary criticism and translation, and research-based scholarly works in both the languages. She also translates between both languages, in both directions. But her fiction and plays she has written so far in Bengali only. Ketaki opines: "there are those sceptics who hold the view that there can be no such identity as that of a serious bilingual writer. They say you cannot be deemed a proper writer until you have written a novel in English. According to them, being a bilingual creator in poetry and scholarly books is not enough. To show your mettle as a writer you must produce English-language fiction; nothing else will do. So discrimination is a many-headed monster, as in mythological narratives. You may cut off one of its heads, but another one will grow in its place. It is really a strategy for the consolidation of power." Therefore her writing career is one of continuous struggle to make her mark in literary world and leave a legacy behind.

Ketaki Kushari Dyson has been writing poetry since childhood and getting them published in Bengali magazines. It is only after she settled in England on a permanent basis that she started writing poetry in English as is evident in her own words."A combination of circumstances gradually conspired to shape me as a bilingual poet. I was living my adult life amongst people who spoke English as a mother tongue; my children were growing up, and English was the language of my new home; I was interacting with the other young mothers whose children were going to the same school as mine. The natural poet in me felt the need to express myself at a deeper level in English."Ms. Dyson belongs to that small family of poets who write original poetry in two languages. According to her in case of poetry, she has two mother tongues. She considers it a privilege of her life to be able to publish poetry in the little magazines of two distinct cultures, thus being in touch with the poetic pulse and "grassroots" in each. According to Professor Sumana Das Sur if "one studies Ketaki's published poetry collections chronologically – *Bolkol* ('Bark'), *Sap-Wood, Sabeej Prithibi* ('The Seeded Earth'), *Jaler Koridor Dhorey* ('Along the Corridor of Water'), *Spaces I Inhabit, Katha Boltey Dao* ('Allow Me To Speak'), *Jadukar Prem, Jadukar Mrityu*('Love the Magician, Death the Magician'), *Memories of Argentina and Other Poems, Dolonchampay Phul Phutechhey* ('The Ginger Lily Has

Blossomed'), *In That Sense You Touched It* – the outward aspects and intimate details of her evolving mental world and the world of her experiences gradually become clear to the eye. Her diasporic position is implicit in the body of her poetry in symbolic patterns. "For instance, several poems spread over more than one collection shows how a Dolonchapa plant (ginger lily)taken by her from India blossomed in a foreign land amidst inclement weather which was not even conducive for its survival. The poem makes us think of a similar struggle of the diasporic poet to pursue her literary endeavor in a distant land. The "Dolon Chapa" plant becomes a symbol of the literary spirit of the poet that is desirous to get out of its cocoon and shake off the inhibitions it initially had.The poet's frustration, her anger, the monologue inside her psyche and the intermittent dialogue that she had with the plant make us realize that it is not just blossoming of a plant rather an evolution of a soul in a foreign land that the poet eagerly waits for. When the first bud appears on the ginger lily twelve years after it has rooted itself in the soil of the new country, the poet sees in it "an extension of her self, an expression of her own being."

In general the term Diaspora refers to the people dispersed from their homeland all over the world. It can be a problematic experience in some way but it can also be an enriching experience. Due to her marriage with an English man Ms. Dyson has spent a long time in Britain than in any other country. She had come in close contact with both the Bengali community and the English. In a seminar arranged by Brick Lane Circle, Ms. Dyson once recounted that one can be members of two different groups and still be faithful to one's roots. "The more multi-dimensional you are the more interesting your work will be. You have to think of the whole of humanity. That is Tagore's message also.

Tagore is also against narrow nationalism."Therefore the experiences that she gathered in the foreign land provided her with food for thought. In the UK, she re-initiated her writing career on an ironing board her physicist husband had made especially for her to iron sarees. Encouraged by Bengali novelist Romapodo Chowdhury she began writing her first ever semi - autobiographical novel *Noton Noton Payraguli* (Those Crested pigeons) serialized in *Desh* in 1981-82 and published as a book in 1983. She wrote for the distant public who may not have a clear picture of the details of life abroad." I didn't think I was capable of writing a novel, but once I was back in Kidlington, I decided to accept the challenge. The elm-trees were dying of what came to be known as the 'elm-tree disease'. Sitting by the back bedroom window, watching the dead and dying elms, I decided that I would have a go at writing a novel. No harm in trying, was there? ,Ketaki stated flatly.While searching for a convincing structure of her first novel, her doctoral thesis which later became a book called *A Various Universe: The Journals and Memoirs of British Men and Women in the Indian Subcontinent,1765-1856.*, proved to be a great help. In her doctoral thesis at Oxford, she had to go through and analyze diaries of British men and women .This thesis of Ketaki provided her with a solid framework of her first novel. The novel "Noton Noton Payragui" interwoven with diaries and letters is regarded by many as the first distinctly 'diasporic' novel in the contemporary sense in the Bengali language. The name of the novel borrowed from the first line of a Bengali nursery rhyme, brings every Bengali back to his/her childhood.The novel is set in an imaginary English location named Norton Hill, halfway between a village and a town, The novel unfolds life of Noton Das, a Bengali woman living in Norton Hill with her husband, Atin Das and two young sons, Topu and Jopu.The novel begins with Noton's letter to her mother, in India, giving her every detail of her daily chores. She does not forget to mention how Jopu has appreciated her mother' s gardening skill by writing a poem on her garden, how she is trying to motivate her children to learn guitar, how she is using an electric blender to paste onion, which in India was an arduous job. Interestingly within the first chapter, Dyson implants the essence of diaspora when she recounts how she has collected seeds from India and planted at the land of Britain. Every letter that Noton writes to her relatives in India makes clear her earnest effort to keep in close touch with them.In letters to her friends and realtives, she also makes a comparative study of socio-political life of England and that of India.In one of her lettersNoton reflects how she struggles to make the British understand the problem of rampant theft of registered letters in India on which exquisite stamps of foreign countries were attached. Interestingly Noton also wonders to see how the not so literate but efficient employees of English Postal System are multitasking with ease and expertise which was rare in the part of India where she was born and brought up.Noton shows an incredible inclination to assimilate to other cultures, as is clear in her experiments with food or in her choice of friends. Instead of avoidance or feeling shy she is friends with her neighbours belonging to different religions and cultures She not only befriends Erica of Irish origin, Fatima from Algeria but also consciously and at times subconsciously imbibes their cultures. Noton invites her friends at home, prepares multi-cuisine foods and keeps socializing in the world where she has settled in after her marriage. Interestingly, in one hand she mixes with her friends belonging to different cultures, on the other she embraces more and more her native language through writing. In an interview in Kolkata literary meet,2016 Ketaki affirmed that if she is in diaspora she has to look at the sunny things of life, she has to make the most of it and enjoy writing about the altogether new experiences. If you are outside your native place where you are born, you have to make continuous adjustments, that obviously gives you a push and a pull and makes you think. If you are a person who is inclined to think, you can make it a sort of strategic advantage for yourself. That is what pushes you into becoming a multicultural and see the lives of different groups of people and to seek out adequate means of expression for that. Noton shares same perspective of Ketaki and shows tremendous zeal to learn new things. Noton is also well received by her neighbours and often becomes a passive listener of the pains and suffering of the women of her group. She also reflects on the life of people of different cultures,how women of different cultures are going through the same turbulence and turmoil in their lives,how the "Lilith" inside women of different cultures are behaving more or less in the same way against the injustice meted out to them by male chauvinistic society, how they are trying to find their space, earn their living, trying to get the respect that they as human beings deserve..The novel becomes a time capsule in its true sense because of the way it tries to capture the natural, social and political milieu of England as well as that of India during a specific span of time.On the one hand, it depicts the disease of elm trees, how she is taking care of English seasonal flowers, how her daily life is affected by the inflation in England, on the other is making statements on the social and political life of India.

The negative side of migrating from a third world country is reflected in the repeated rejection of Noton's job applications in different universities in England. In spite of having extremely good qualifications as a student of English literature and even after earning a Ph.D. from The University of Oxford she was rejected on multiple grounds such as she was a woman, she was a married woman, she was a married woman with two small children, and she was a person of Indian ethnic origin. Therefore she has to find some other alternative to nurture her scholarly self. So she together with an English friend become the organizer of poetry reading workshops and encourages people of different cultures to join it. She curiously observes here that poetry reading workshops which are very much common in Calcutta are a much rare event in England. Instead of feeling secure in her cocoon Noton is found to try her hand in different new things which makes us realize that diaspora also represents a multicultural possibility. It also gives one scope to borrow from multicultures. It helps one to be an heir to all cultures, not any particular culture. That opens a tremendous amount of possibility to shape one's own identity. This is clear from the fact that she is trying to grasp other languages and cultures as well. She is also aware of the sense of alignment that this diasporic condition entails. The claustrophobic sense of cultural vacuum that one experiences while migrating from one's homeland, a sense of lack of identity, a painful uprooting from Bengali cultural milieu and family is also very much clear in Noton's diaries.

In another masterpiece *Nari, Nogori* Ms. Dyson has very skilfully encapsulated the global issues in her native language. The plot revolves around Tatyana, who is Rush-Armenian by birth but brought up in Paris. She is a free-spirited woman who does not want to be confined in typical mould of a Russian lady that everyone else expects her to be. She even hates the way her Russian landlady wants her to sustain her Russian customs and cultures in English soil. Neither she prefers the variety of coffee which is favourite of the Russians. She has even commented that it is hypocrisy to be loyal to one's own culture and abhor the culture of the country helping you to earn your bread. In Tatyana, we find a rootless conservative soul who is in search of her own identity. Ketaki observes that though she claims herself to be orthodox, she is basically an agnostic. We can find a real dichotomy in her character. Though she does not like nationalist fervour shown by the emigrants, she is also unhappy about the fact that they are of the last generation of emigrants who will be speaking in Russian because the next generation is hardly taking any interest in their native language.

In Tatyana's conversation with the writer we come to know that while living in Paris she fell in love with an Afghan young man. Her love for that person belonging to a different culture as well as religion was so intense that she was even ready to give up her own religion though she knew it very well that his religion and culture are very different from hers and the status of woman in his country is totally different from that of Paris. The love affair did not result in marriage because he was going to take a job in the government office where he was not allowed to have a bride of foreign origin. Now he was like any other Afghan man who loves his country much more than his lover. That ended Tatyana's hope of getting married to him. As the saying goes in spite of everything life moves on. Tatyana found her new love interest in a French boy who fell head over heels love with her. Still, Tatyana could not make up her mind about marriage. Therefore she distanced herself from his French lover and took up a job in Oxford so that she can get time to realize the exact nature of the relationship she was sharing with him. .Coming to Oxford Tatyana shifts her attention to another English guy with whom she shares some common interest.

The man cynical about any romantic relationship wants to be physical with her to which she does not agree. Later she repents and thinks probably being physical can be the first step of germination of love between a man and a woman. According to Tololyan(2012) "'Dispersion' is the more general and inclusive term, whereas 'diaspora' is merely one of several kinds of dispersion so that, in a curious reversal, it has become a synecdoche, the part - diaspora - standing for the whole. Other forms of mobility and dispersion include migration intended to acquire education, jobs, land, settlement, new citizenship, or a combination thereof; there are also mobile traders and itinerant labourers who circulate between homeland and extraterrestrial opportunities ; there are victims of mass deportations, refugees and asylum seekers - some choose mobility, others have it thrust upon them; some are uprooted, others uproot themselves. Some eventually return home, many are assimilated, and the remainder may become consolidated into diaspora communities."Tatyana is one such diasporic character who is a citizen in her 'new' home country," possesses a hybrid culture and identity or at the very least has developed a comfortable bicultural competence. She is a diasporic because of a set of cumulative decisions to continue to remain bi- or multi-local, to care about others in the diaspora with whom she shares an ethnodiasporic origin, and also to care in some manner about the well-being of the homeland of the ancestors."

The plot of Ketaki's third novel, *Jol Phunre Aagun* (2003, 'Fire Piercing Through Water') alternates between two places-Calcutta and a town near London. Anjan, an NRI, living in the UK discovers that the vision of one of his eyes has deteriorated after an operation. His English wife Jane took him to the hospital and get him admitted to the emergency section of the ophthalmology department. Two different diasporic phenomenon are shared by two characters, a Bengali NRI of mixed parentage and his more mixed daughter. While in hospital Anjan recalls memories of the past and reflects on socio-political life of England. During that period his Daughter, Milita was staying in Kolkata. We come to know from the monologue Milita shares how she experiences a feeling of confusion after moving to the cultural environment in Kolkata which is entirely different from the country where she was brought up.

Rabindranath o Victoria Ocampor Sandhaney. is a research-based scholarly novel on the two famous personalities, our very own Tagore andthe lynchpin of Argentina's intellectual scene, Victoria Ocampo. Ketaki has claimed to have conducted the most extensive investigations into Tagore's Argentine adventure and his interaction with Victoria Ocampo. That Victoria Ocampo was one remarkable woman of the twentieth century was first revealed after publication of Doris Meyer's first full-length English-language biography named *Victoria Ocampo: Against the Wind and the Tide.* This book made Ketaki realize thatvVictoria Ocampo deserved to be known and studied in her own right and not just as Tagore's Muse. It spurred her on to discover this enigmatic persona. With renewed determination to explore the world of Victoria Ocampo Ketaki began to learn Spanish so that she could read Ocampo's work in the original. She realized then that of all the gifted and attractive women with whom Tagore had come into direct contact in his long life Ocampo had possibly been the most distinguished. When her own long life and its work are considered in their entirety, she is the closest to him in stature. Ketaki reviewed Doris Meyer's biography of Ocampo for the Bengali quarterly *Jijnasa* . As Bengali scholars were unaware of Ocampo's obituary essay on Tagore, written immediately after his death in 1941, she translated it into Bengali and published it in *Jijnasa* too. She then discovered an important cache of letters in an English archival collection which revealed to her that there was much more to the Tagore-Ocampo story than the Bengali intellectuals had realized. Ketaki's first archival findings on the subject and fragments of translation from Ocampo's essays were incorporated by her into the body of the book she wrote in Bengali in 1981-82 in a mixed genre, pioneering the mixture of fiction and non-fiction within the same work. In this book, entitled *Rabindranath o Victoria Ocampor Sandhane* ('In search of Rabindranath Tagore and Victoria Ocampo'), she interwove fiction with research and translation work, giving her own work to the heroine of her novel, Anamika.

As the plot of the novel unfolds we find that Anamika, the researcher is consulting data scattered in different books and journals and unpublished letters exchanged between these two eminent persons to find out the exact nature of the relationship between Tagore and Victoria. It was the Nobel Prize for literature to Tagore that made Tagore's encounter with Victoria Ocampo possible. The Nobel Prize made Tagore internationally famous. English versions of his works were re-translated into many other languages and he started receiving invitations from many countries which gave him the scope to travel widely, have foreign friends, and meet many other distinguished personalities of his time which helped him to grow even further. "Victoria Ocampo was an ardent admirer of Tagore's works, which she could read in English, French, and Spanish versions. While the intensity with which she greeted his works was a very personal gesture of hers, deriving its vivid colours from her private life, it was, at the same time, a part of the widespread enthusiasm for Tagore that prevailed in Latin America at that time",Ketaki stated.It was Andre Gide's French re-translation of *Gitanjali*, , in 1914, that made her aware of Tagore's works. She was going through a crisis in her personal life. She has a failed marriage and she was hopelessly in love with Martinez. She was so overwhelmed with emotions that she wept after going through the pages of *Gitanjali*. According to Ketaki"It was like an act of recognition, a release, a liberation. She recognized her own intense emotions in the mystical yearnings of the poems and at the same time found a deep spiritual comfort in it. "She began to read Tagore in translation, whatever was available, in English, French, or Spanish, with intense hunger.

Besides the mesmerizing character of Victoria the character of Anamika does not fail to stand out. The novel unveils that she was a student of comparative literature. Now she is living in Britain with her psychiatrist husband Ranjan. She helps her children with their French or German homework, she enthusiastically learns foreign languages, she appreciates the lyrical appeal of folk songs from different countries with equal fervour and at the same time does not hesitate to take part in experimental trials in the hospital where her husband Ranjan works. As she proceeds with her research work on Tagore and Ocampo her own personal life undergoes a deep crisis. But she denies succumbing to this intense pressure. After Ranjan dies from a terrorist attack she feels temporarily disoriented, but she recovers soon. She decides to bring up her children in Britain with her head held high. According to Cohen(1996) the Jewish tradition of the diaspora can very simply be called the victim tradition where all of whom experienced traumatic interludes in their histories which led to their dispersion or further dispersion.All scholars of diasporas recognize that the victim tradition is at the core of any definition of the concept of diaspora. Yet even if it is necessary to take full account of this tradition, it is also necessary to transcend it. It can hardly be denied that for all the victim diasporas, their experiences in modern nation-states have been fearful as well as enriching. Cohen(1996) further comments that the Jews' considerable intellectual and spiritual achievements simply could not have been possible if they would have confined themselves in a narrow tribal society like Judea. The Armenians and the Irish thrived materially and politically when they came to settle in the 'land of opportunity', the USA. Similarly, the Palestinians are more prosperous and better-educated than the locals in the countries of their exile, while those of African descent in the diaspora have made contributions in the field of the performing arts,music, painting, sculpture, and literature. The character of Anamika testifies to this statement too.As the novel progresses we see how the entire personality of Anamika sublimates with every new experience she has in her life in the foreign soil, with every person of a different culture and religion she meets and has interaction with.

The story of Emilia, another free-spirited woman in the novel unfolds world history. She was born in Turkey into a Sephardic Jewish family,. Emilia's life-long rootlessness due to her Sephardic Jewish background forced her to travel from one country to another. Being a part of minority family all through her life Emilia had to experience a sense of insecurity, uncertainty, anxiety, a feeling of embarrassment. According to Tololyan "Diasporas need not apologize for their alleged lack of authenticity, for the hybridity of diasporan identity, as if it represented mere decline from some purer homeland form. ...The stateless power of diasporas lies in their heightened awareness of both the perils and rewards of multiple belonging and in their sometimes exemplary grappling with the paradoxes of such belonging, which is increasingly the condition that non-diasporan nationals also face in the transnational era." The novel shows how Emilia overcomes the periods of intense suffering in her life and how her life acquires a new meaning, a new dimension through her acquaintance with Anamika, with whom she shares a common world view.

Writing plays as an activity Ketaki came at a matured age. According to her playwriting is especially problematic. Unless you happen to have a group of friends near you, for putting up those plays you have to depend on your distant contacts. In a seminar arranged by Brick Lane Circle Ketaki recounts that there is a complicated connection between the media with which we write and the message that is to be conveyed. It was easier for her to focus in Bengali for debating social life. Bengali reflects a more gregarious and inclusive kind of society. It has a number of kinship terms, different kinds of nephews, nieces and all. To some extent, the media shapes the message. But to depict a new kind of reality which is not covered by the writers' home we sometimes adopt the techniques of intercultural mediation so that we can portray the details of new reality with greater subtlety. If you add the dimension of time you will realize that no society is static. Our country of origin as it is now is not the country we left. There are continuities as well as discontinuities. For her, the best strategy has been to depict life as she sees around her or record narratives that her friends relate to her.

In order to describe how she came to write plays, Ketaki mentions that a senior friend associated with Calcutta's group theatre movement used to ask her to write plays which will depict the contemporary world. The writer was in doubt whether she had the capacity to construct a play. The writer had experience of acting though.In her childhood she along with her sister used to hang curtains and dance on "taktaposh".She used to incorporate and improvise dialogues in it also. She had also watched some "yatras "and puppet shows in her childhood. While in school she witnessed plays of different eminent actors. She also took part in a few plays in school where they used to make costumes out of georgette sarees of their mothers. At the age of 14, she joined Lady Brabourne college where she had the opportunity to experience a few dance dramas by Tagore. She performed in a few Sanskrit plays as well. During her student life in Presidency college, she had Sanskrit as pass subject. To study Sanskrit the students had to go to Sanskrit college. During that period Ketaki went through a no of famous Sanskrit plays like Avigyan Shakuntalam, Mrichakatika, etc. During her stay in Oxford, she had seen many live performances of English and European plays. The experiences that she gathered over the years spurred her growth as a playwright.

Ketaki has constructed three plays: *Raater Rode* (*Night's Sunlight* ,premièred in 1994, published in 1997), *Mozart Chocolate*(published in 1998), and *Suparnarekha* (published in 2002)..For her play *Raater rode* she set the scene in a Bengali dining room .There is a play within play sequence.The play addressed some serious issues like" sati".menstruation, hysterectomy, global warming and climate change In the Introduction to her English translation of *Night's Sunlight* (2000), she shares a glimpse into her diasporic self by stating,"Thus, I do not consider that this play of mine is really a 'foreign' play for this country. How could it be, when it is set in a living-room in Britain? But what is more, whoever reads this play will realize that it could not have been written by someone who did not live here. Like virtually everything I have written in my adult life, it belongs in a very real sense to Britain, of which I have been a citizen since 1965, and where I live and work for most of the time. It is British writing - but with a difference, because it is written in Bengali, which links it to another cultural matrix, makes it part of a distant literary/socio-cultural 'polysystem'. In effect, like most work I produce in any genre, it has two cultural matrices."She further writes,"Bengalis can see that my play is 'Bengali-but-with-a-difference'. Those who see themselves as the moral guardians of theatre criticism may not take to it as ducks to water, but with their feet kicking, they may admit that at least it fits conveniently into the slot of eccentric diasporic writing. Others perceive that it has an international flavour without losing its Bengali pulse. I want to show my British friends that the same text can also be read as 'British-but-with-a-difference'.Due to the length of the play the writer could not decide whom should she ask to tackle such a long and complex play. Professor Sunil Das, a director of Theatre group "Somdatto "offered to take it on. The writer heard that there will be a drama festival in Manchester in 1994. With the staging of *Raater Rode,* it was the first time premier of Calcutta group theatre happened in Manchester.

In 1998 her second play *Mozart Chocolate* was published in the annual issue of Desh.*Mozart Chocolate* depict that on a rainy day Ila, a Bengali woman living in England, is folding and rearranging the saris that have been accumulated over the years in her wardrobe. Her friend Lipi arrives and they confer about various contemporary issues. Lipi leaves while Ila continues to arrange her saris, .Interestingly, in Mozarts chocolate each saree either from pre-migration or post migration life brings back memories., associations,friendships,.The tidiness of a wardrobe leads to tell us about the formation of an identity. When she speaks to figures from her past who emerge from behind her wardrobe we can catch a glimpse of different facets of Bengal's social and political history .In the last scene Ila discovers that the house where she had beautiful memories of her childhood has been demolished for the erection of a highrise. The play shows how in spite of life's unexpected turns, chocolates become a symbol of life's comfort.

It is an ambitious effort on my part to explore and comment on the literary world of the diasporic writer, Ketaki Kushari Dyson. Being a Bengali I had the privilege of going through the wealth of creative work she offered to Bengali literature. Here I have tried to analyze to the best of my ability how many of her writings in her native language portray the life long struggle of the diasporic population in other countries and how the story of her own struggle in a foreign land and the subsequent process of cultural assimilation has been repeatedly reflected in the bulk of her masterpieces.

Works Cited

1. Dyson, Ketai. K. "A Scrapboook of Memories and Reflections". Parabaas.com, Sep 2017. https://www.parabaas.com/translation/database/translations/essays kkd_memoir_ch4.html
2. Dyson,Ketaki.K ." Ketaki Kushari Dyson on Poetry -- Kolkata Literary Meet 2016". *YouTube,* youtube/0ghZ0izB2lA.
3. Dyson, Ketaki.K. Writing plays in Bengali in the Diaspora: My Experiences - By Ketaki Kushari Dyson. *YouTube,* uploaded by Brick Lane Circle,29 Dec.2014, https://youtu.be/NVoTFYqMgMY
4. Prakash, Anand. Diaspora Writing. *YouTube,* https://youtu.be/qPGKar9yEs8
5. Sur,Sumana.D. "Two Women Writers of the Bengali Diaspora:Ketaki Kushari Dyson and Dilara Hashem". *Parabaas.com,* Mar.2011.

https://www.parabaas.com/translation/database/translations/essays/pSumana.html

6. Tölölyan, Khachig, "Rethinking *Diaspora*(s): Stateless Power in the Transnational Moment". *Diaspora.vol.* 5.no.1,1996,pp.7-8. http://readinglists.ucl.ac.uk/items/842B0968-D5B9-4D3F-7135-417244E0FE2A.html
7. Tololyan, Khachig."Diaspora studies: Past, present, and promise".*IMI Working Papers Series*,no.55,Apr. 2012,pp.55https://www.academia.edu/28876043/Diaspora_studies_Past_present_and_promise

SIGNS OF NOSTALGIA AND SCHIZOPHRENIA IN ANITA DESAI'S *BYE BYE BLACKBIRD*

Dr. S. Lingeswari
Assistant Professor of English
Mannar Thirumalai Naicker College, Madurai

In these days, people move from country to country in order to have a better fortune in their life. Though they may have reasons for their emigration, the new alienated surrounding leaves them with the signs of nostalgia. Their shift from their land doesn't only separate them from their relations but also from their own selves. Writers too record such signs in their works. The immigrants are left with a high level of stress which leads them to confusion, irritation, rage as it is observed by Ortega Y. Gasset:

> … The other man also has his here but this here of the other is not mine. Our 'heres are mutually exclusive, they are not inter penetrable, they are different, with the result that the perspective in which the world appears to him always different from mine. Hence, our worlds do not adequately coincide. For the present I am in mine, and he is in his. And this is a fresh reason for radical solitude. Not only am I outside of his; we are mutually two outsiders (fueras) and hence radically strangers.' (Wandrekar 1)

Erich Fromm in his theory about the human pathology believes that a man is filled with reason and imagination. The man is not satisfied with the basic needs and has an appetite for progress. Either for material satisfaction or thirst for knowledge, he is ready to leave his homeland. It is highly questionable whether he could achieve his goal with dignity in the adopted nation. William James defines that if a man immigrates to an alien country, he stands like an outsider at the edge of a 'pain threshold'. In his Varieties of Religious Experience, William James states it as: a 'pain threshold', a 'fear threshold', and a 'misery threshold'.

Many Indo- English writers prefer to settle in the Western countries. The west always attracts the people of East. In the case of writers, the West provides them an apt opportunity to enjoy literary affluence and material advancement. The Indian born diaspora writers like Salman Rushdie, V.S. Naipaul, Anita Desai, Bharati Mukherjee, Shashi Tharoor, Amitav Gosh, Vikram Seth, Sunethra Gupta, Rohinton Mistry, Jumpha Lahiri, Hari Kunzru contributed much to Indian English Literature. The word diaspora is derived from Greek and means 'scatter'. The term, when applied to human beings, means the scatter of people when are away from their native land. A vast interest is shown in cultural studies and the works written by the writers of the Indian diaspora: "Language and cultures are transformed as they come into contact with the other languages and cultures. Diasporic writing raises questions regarding the definitions of 'home' and 'nation'. Schizophrenia and nostalgia are often the preoccupations of these writers as they seek to locate themselves in new cultures. It becomes important to question the nature of their relationship with the work of writers and literatures of the country of their origin and to examine the different strategies they adopt in order to negotiate the cultural space of the countries of their adoption" (Jain 113). The novelists like Anita Desai, Bharati Mukherjee, Kamala Markandaya and so on settled in foreign countries as well as recorded the experiences of the displaced. Displacement is one of the causes that affect the normalcy of an individual. The displaced is ailed of schizophrenia. Anita Desai's *Bye Bye Blackbird,* in her words, is a significant study of Schizophrenia.

Schizophrenia is a type of mental disorder which affects an individual's thoughts, actions, expressions, emotions, realization of reality and the relationship with the others. It is different from other mental disorders. The people affected from schizophrenia cannot be much deviated from the common moody natured. It is difficult to realize at the outset. These people have problems in maintaining relationships, doing well in the society and in the working atmosphere. At times, they shall be deviated from reality. Their attitude reflects their confused thoughts and images and shocking behaviour. The symptoms of schizophrenia includes: talk without making sense, move quickly from one to the other thought without a logical connection, inability in taking decisions, forgetting or losing things, problems in making sense in routine sights, sounds and feelings, trouble in paying attention and so on. The major characters Adit Sen, Dev and Sarah are seen with this mental illness in a way or other. Most of the symptoms of their illness are resulted with the effects of becoming alienated from their country, culture and relations. These characters live in attractive landscape, nuances of nostalgia, moments of tension and torment. They are captured between the two: repelling isolation, attraction of togetherness. They have to choose between the two which they fail to do. This failure and the resulted dilemma is rooted in their psyche.

Anita Desai, originally named Anita Mazumdar was born to a German mother and a Bengali father and spent her days in Delhi. She has authored novels and short stories. Most of her novels are with her personal life or her personal influence. Her themes are ranging from anti- sentimentalism to Western quintessential ideologies of India. Her novel *Bye Bye Blackbird* analyses the immigrants' psychology who suffer from the mixed feelings of love and hatredness of both their own and the land they adopted. Blackbird, in the title symbolizes the immigrants from India, whom are greeted 'goodbye' by the West. The characters prove the fact how the immigrants undergo conflicts in an alien country. Through this novel, the novelist explores the lives of the immigrants who are seeking a new identity in the adopted nation. This book, in its theme, is divided into three parts: (i) Arrival - starts with the arrival of Dev in London from India (ii) Discovery and Recognition – the major characters Adit Sen and Dev recognized their position and opportunity in the adopted nation and discovered their interest and inner selves (iii) Departure – at the end of the discovery and recognition Adit Sen departs to his mother land. The story is set in England with the contrast thoughts, emotions, feelings and background of India.

Dev, recently shifted to London, is attracted with the new land. He comes to London with the intention of continuing his higher studies. But in the adopted nation he is no more seen with the passion in education. Only a few days of his visit to London, he announces of the purpose of his alienation. In a few days, he has completely forgotten about continuation of his higher education. In his mind, there exist the symptoms of Schizophrenia. He is attracted with the alien country through his writings and imagination. Though he is attracted by the new place, he is affected with nostalgia, and he feels himself as a stranger: "Nothing in his past twenty- two years had resembled remotely this world he had entered by stepping through the door of the King's Arms" (BBB 12). When he is denied to be announced the cost of a painted duck, he is suffered from a mental ache. He compares the lifestyle and attitude of people in London with that of his own. It is transparent when he compares the life of Laurel Lane with that of India. Unlike India, Laurel Lane is completely silent and invisible. Everyone in this alien country lives hidden as a stranger. He is confused with the contrast ideas of staying in the new nation and leaving it. His mental ailment becomes transparent in his immaturity in choosing his future, in his commercial mindedness and pleasure seeking attitude. As it is opined by Bertrand Russell in his essay *Can We Keep Open Mind?*, the young ones are of highly open-minded because of unsteadiness in any a field firmly. That's what the thing is seen in the decision of Dev to continue his education in the West. His mental conflict is presented by the writer as "He is perfectly aware of schizophrenia that is inflecting him like the disease to which all Indians abroad, he declares, are prone. At times he invites it, at times he fights it. He is not sure what it might be like to be one himself, in totality. He is not sure. Any longer" (BBB 86).

Dev is seen with the mental illness with the effects identity crisis and his life in alienation. His mental conflict is clear by his social disorientation. He feels isolated even when living with his wife in his own flat. At once when he returns to his flat he feels as isolated and is dumb with dispair: "Adit stood in the hall, blinking, not recognizing his cat or his home exactly like a stranger arrived at a hotel in a strange city" (BBB 205). He is no longer continued in his identity than a label- 'a wog', 'asiatic', or 'indian immigrant'. He gets psychic: "He had a dreadful vision of himself in the white shirt and shuffling slippers of a lunatic's garb at an asylum, an outsider not only by virtue of his colour but by an imagination run amuck" (BBB 217).

Adit and Dev represent two types of immigrants. To both, England means different things. Adit believes that he leads the English lifestyle. But unknowingly he lives only as an Indian. It is transparent in his purchase of ingredients, the recipes he asks his wife to cook and so on. He chooses the alien country whole heartedly, marries an English girl and wants to continue his life in England. In his profession he is not shared with better fortunes like an Englishman. But he feels happy in England and blames Indians and Indianism. But he is stricken with nostalgia even after stayed for a long in London. His wish to visit India on a holiday for over a month and the list of desires to do in India proves his nostalgic signs. He is the kind to be with an illusion on the West as the land with golden opportunity. Dev is the type of an immigrant who is conscious of his alienation and inability to imbibe the new nation's culture. He is more sensitive than Adit in his relationship with the English. He loves England and also hates it with all his heart. He suffers from, as opined by R.S. Sharma, 'Caliben complex', who says thus: "In his often mutually contradictory responses to England, Dev displays characteristic psychic traits of an ex- colonial. He suffers essentially from a Caliban complex, now adoring, now loathing, the sensibility that he has imbibed from the colonial rule" (Sharma 31).

Sarah, the English wife of Adit, also suffers from alienation though lives in her own land. By marrying an Indian, she is not recognized from her fellow- countrymen. She is weak and submissive. She is the victim of values and culture. She is an outsider in the Indian community too where she is married because being an English. She has lost her identity without displaced. In her inner self there is a conflict between the role of an English woman and as an Indian wife. She is fascinated to India. Her image of India is that of a tourist. Only at the end, she moves to India and is yet to face the real India. It is she who has given up her more to the marriage. Though Adit disdains India and wants to be English, he remains an Indian in his food habits, favourite music and in the remembrance of India. But it is only Sarah who changes herself from her English culture and lifestyle. She cooks Indian foods, reads about India, listens to Indian music and at the end her departure to India makes it clear of her departure from her own self. She plays two roles: (i) maintaining ledgers at school (ii) Indian wife. At once, she realizes her alienation from her own individuality: "Her face was only a mask, her body only a costume. Where was Sarah? Staring out of the window at the chimney tops and the clods, she wondered if Sarah had any an existence at all, and then she wondered, with great sadness, if she would ever be allowed to step off the stage, leave the theatre and enter the real world whether English or Indian" (BBB 36)

Anita Desai has highlighted the immigrant experience in her contrast citation of the background. One of the important references is the contrast lies in the landscapes of India and England. Adit feels Indian landscape as dry and barren. His view towards Indian landscape symbolizes the lack of opportunity. Only following the week end in his in- laws, he recognizes the stark beauty of India: "The long, lingering twilight of the English summer trembling over the garden had seemed to him like an invalid stricken with anemia, had aroused in him a sudden clamour, like a child's tantrum, to see again an Indian sunset, its wild conflagration, rose and orange, flamingo pink and lemon, scattering into a million sparks in the night sky"(BBB 202). To Sarah, India is a land of warmth and mystery which is naturally a thought of a tourist. Even the thought of Indian heat and dust seems exotic to her. Dev is inspired by the landscape of England. Though he is unimpressed with the city London at the beginning with the concepts like tube station, dead silence but inspired by the countryside of England. He decides to stay in England when he discovers the attraction of the English countryside.

The longing for their homeland is seen when the immigrants have gathered at one place to frame their own club. The Indian music played by the Indian troupe mesmerized them. They are attracted by the music as they feel it being in homeland: "We are strangers here. It is so long since we have heard our own music. To listen it to have our own Indian sun shining in us again warming our frozen blood…" (BBB 97). Indian's punctuality in time- keeping is also discussed. Unlike the English, Indians never follow time. Following time is very important and at the same time, these displaced believe that in following time as everywhere and every situation won't be better. They believe that if a human being continues to follow the routines on time, it can't be natural.

Dev leaves India with the intention of freeing himself from the social and economic bondage. After entering into the new place, he can be self- sufficient. But there in his mind is always a thought as he is uncared by anyone and his mind is longing to return: "where somebody cares for me. Sugar is sweet and so is she" (BBB 21). He compares and relates everything whatever he sees and experiences in the new nation with that of his own. When he sees the high streets of London, he finds the echoes of Himalayan Mall. He tries to relate the commonness in nature and finds solace. The thing that hurts him most in the alien country is the indifference of people and pets. Throughout he is confronted with the buildings in the new nation not with the human beings. Adit is haunted by nostalgia when he stays at his in- laws. He interprets the things he sees and hears with the Indian context. The nostalgia forces him to escape from the adopted country to his own. He wants to escape to the nation from which he had escaped earlier. The battle he fights so far is lost. He has made his mind to return to India because the latter guarantees him love, respect, care and security. He realized, though England is a heaven, India as a real heaven for himself.

The immigrants Dev and Adit are of wonder, surprise and adventure at the beginning but give way to them as get experienced. Then they feel fear, anxiety, longing for the past, memories of homeland. At the end, they take refuge in nostalgia and dreams. The immigrant's inability to adapt with the new country creates a space mentally, psychologically and spiritually from him. Adit represents the Indian immigrants who are attracted by the glamour and financial prospects of England but are at the end frustrated and isolated because of the bitter practical experience. This bitter practical experience makes the blackbird to transform into a homing bird. He is longing for his homeland: "No- England! England. I've done with England now, Sarah, I'm going back… To India?... To India… Home" (BBB 231). Contrarily, Sarah wants to fit herself and her baby into the pattern of her husband's life. She is shocked to find her husband's gradual lack of interest and sympathy in her. In her mind, there has been desire to withdraw herself from the British society to the life of India. A conflict in Sarah is her marriage to Adit. She married him because of her grace and interest towards India. But whenever there comes a discussion among her colleagues at school about her Indian husband and future life, she avoids them. Instead, she prefers to listen to the boring talks of the teachers even for hours. It leaves the teachers in the school think, "If she's ashamed of having an Indian husband, why did she go and marry him"? (BBB 39). She is with psychic anguish between allegiance and love and at the end withdraws from her English self. Her psychological problems emerge from her cross cultural union. As opined by Usha Bande:

Sarah is overwhelmed by the change because she cannot fully immerse herself in her husband's culture, nor can she adapt herself to her own society. Normally within our own community each of us has a unified self. Cultural values give us this specific identity. But under certain pressures, the personality may break up and different selves spring up. Ven de Berge prefers to call it 'Sociosis' rather than 'neurosis' when socio- historical alterations affect the psychology of an individual. Sarah's dual estrangement comes, not from social transformation within her society, but from a cross- cultural catalysis of her own choice. (Bande 122)

The blackbird symbolically represents all human beings who are trapped in a world where choices are almost impossible to make use of. The author also narrates the motifs of the immigrants' journey and departure to prove their quest for identity and intellectual growth. Anita Desai proves that an immigrant is aware of his alienation and the state of being unwanted. He has a choice to return to the place where he is wanted and can be one with. But the choice is to be taken by him.

Anita Desai, through this novel, explores the experience of immigrants from the intellectual side. She has presented the dilemma of the immigrants. It suits any coloured migrant in any White foreign country:

> There are days in which the life of an alien appears enthrallingly rich and beautiful to him, and that of a home- body too dull, too stale to return to ever. Then he hears a word in the tube or notices an expression on an English face that overturns his latest decision and, drawing himself together, he feels he can never bear to be the unwanted immigrant but must return to his own land, however abject or dull, where he has, atleast, a place in the sun, security, status and freedom. (BBB 96)

In this novel *Bye Bye Blackbird* Anita Desai gives prominence in exploring her characters' state of mind than the causes of their alienation. She is not only records the Indian immigrants to the West but also vice versa. She highlights both the physical and psychological problems of the Indian immigrants and their difficulty to adjust with the new surroundings. Her characters, their inner conflicts and crisis are true to the context though they are imaginative.

Works Cited

1. Bande, Usha. *The Novels of Anita Desai: A Study in character and Conflict*. New Delhi:
2. Perstiege Books, 1988.
3. Desai, Anita. *Bye Bye Blackbird*. Delhi: Hind Pocket Books, 1971.
4. Fromm, Erich. *The Sane Society*. London: Routledge and Kegan Paul, 1956.
5. Hande, Usha. *The Novels of Anita Desai: A Study in Character and Conflict*. New
6. Delhi: Prestige Books, 1988.
7. Iyengar, K. R. Srinivasa. *Indian Writitng in English*. New Delhi: Sterling, 1964.
8. Jain, Jasbir. *Writers of the Indian Diaspora*. Jaipur: Rawat, 1998.
9. Sharma, R.S. *Anita Desai*. New Delhi: Arnold Heinemann Publishers, 1981.
10. … "Alienation, Accommodation and the Locale in Anita Desai's Bye Bye Blackbird".
11. New Delhi: Arnold Heinemann Publishers, 1981.
12. Wandrekar, Kalpana. "The Ailing Aliens: Anita Desai's Bye- Bye Blackbird: A
13. Symptomatic Study of Schizophrenia" *Image of India in the Indian Novel in English*.
14. Bombay: Orient Longman, 1993.

INDIAN DIASPORA LITERATURE: A BRIEF HISTORICAL ANALYSIS OF CHARACTERISTICS, THEMES AND AUTHORS OF DIASPORIC WRITINGS

Dr Viju M.J,
Asst. Professor, Research & PG Dept. of English
St Thomas College (Autonomous), Thrissur, Kerala
(Affiliated to the University of Calicut)

Introduction

Diasporic or expatriate writing occupies a place of great significance between countries and cultures. Indian Diaspora writers have been at the centre stage in the last decade because of the formulation of theory being generated by these writers. Language and cultures are transformed when these writers are often pre-occupied with the elements of nostalgic feelings locate themselves in new cultures. They always write in relation to the culture of their homeland and negotiate with the cultural space of the host land. By looking at the diasporic literature in a broader perspective it is seen that such literature helps in understanding various cultures, glocalizing the global and even spreading universal peace. Theories are generated and positions defined in order to construct new identities today. This movement causes the dislocation and locations of cultures and individuals harp upon memories. Diasporic writers live on the margins of two countries and create cultural theories.

The Indian Diaspora

The Indian Diaspora is a generic term to describe the people who migrated from territories that are currently within the borders of the Republic of India. It also refers to their descendants. The Diaspora is currently estimated to number over twenty million, composed of "NRIs" (Indian citizens, not residing in India) and "PIOs" (Persons of Indian Origin who have acquired the citizenship of some other country). The Diaspora covers practically every part of the world. There are three categories of overseas Indians: (i) **NRI's:** Indian citizens staying abroad for an indefinite period for whatever purpose (Majority in Gulf);(ii) **PIO's:** Overseas Indian who have become citizens of the countries of their settlement and (iii) **SPIO:** Stateless Person of Indian Origin have no documents to substantiate their Indian Origin (Majority in Myanmar and Sri Lanka).

Meaning and Characteristics of Diaspora

Interestingly, the term 'diaspora', 'exile' alienation', 'expatriation', are synonymous and possess an ambiguous status of being both a refugee and an ambassador. The two roles are different, the diasporic writers attempt at doing justice to both. As a refugee, he seeks security and protection, and as an ambassador projects his own culture and helps enhance its comprehensibility. Migration takes place due to various reasons and in the Indian context the migratory movements were governed by historical, political, economic reasons including higher education, better prospects and marriage.

However, the Indian community has shown a greater sense of adjustments, adaptability, mobility and accessibility. This aspect is brought out very beautifully by Bhiku Parekh who states:

> The diasporic Indian is like the banyan tree, the traditional symbol of the Indian way of life, he spreads out his roots in several soils, drawing nourishment

> from one when the rest dry up. Far from being homeless, he has several homes, and that is the only way he increasingly comes to feel at home in the world (106).

The chief characteristic features of the diasporic writings are the quest for identity, uprooting and re-rooting, insider and outsider syndrome, nostalgia, nagging sense of guilt etc. The diasporic writers turn to their homeland for various reasons. For example, Naipaul, who is on a perpetual quest for his roots turns to India for the same. Rushdie visits India to mythologize its history. Mistry visits and re-visits India for a kind of re-vitalization and to re-energize his aching soul. Bharati Mukherjee's childhood memories haunt her time and again. All the same it is necessary to realise the importance of cultural encounter, the bicultural pulls which finally helps in the emergence of the new culture. The diasporic writings also known as the 'theory of migrancy' helps generate aesthetic evaluation, negotiate with cultural constructs and aid the emergence of a new hybridity.

The Importance of Diaspora to India

The impressive Diaspora has played an important role in promoting India's interest abroad and act as its unnamed ambassadors. This is more so in the fields of culture, education, economic development and health and arts. Indians are leaders in areas like information technology and largely contribute to this. Above all, PIOs can help India by investing in Indian industry and infrastructure to encourage its economic growth. Even though NRI's contribution is not visible, but they are helping their country through varied activities in India. Many reports reveal that NRI's are a major source of Direct Foreign Investment, market development (outsourcing), technology transfer, charity, tourism, political contributions and more substantial flows of knowledge, in India. The NRIs have come forward with several non-governmental organizations in India helping in array of developmental, educational and social projects. It has been observed that a large number of NRIs is actively taking part in several welfare programs in India. They have registered many NGOs to encourage education, health care and developmental activities such as water management, rural development and self-help programs, etc. They are also assisting in social and environmental problems in India.

Diaspora in Science & Other Fields in India

The role of science in the Diaspora needs to be further highlighted. The Diaspora's scientific achievements, in virtually every field, have not just enhanced India's image in the world. They have also led to a direct and mutually-reinforcing synergy between Indian science abroad and at home. This is most visible of course in India's IT sector and its symbiotic relationship with the Silicon Valley in California. Besides, the fear of a "brain drain" is misguided. A "brain" sitting in an uncongenial environment can drain away faster than if it goes to a stimulating interference-free environment abroad. Indian Diaspora has also emerged as an important factor in India's foreign policy, economic development and knowledge transfer. With US $ 56 billion of remittances, overseas Indians play an important role in India's foreign exchange management. The success of Indians in the developed world, particularly in knowledge industries and professions like medicine and academia has transformed India's image. Domestic reaction to the plight of Tamils in Sri Lanka, highlight the implication of a Diaspora factor in our external relations. The LTTE and separatists movements in Punjab illustrate the impact of Diaspora in national security.

History of Indian Diaspora

According to Jain (1993) in the study of Indian Diaspora, it is customary to distinguish between two main phases of emigration: "Overseas emigration in the nineteenth century" and "Twentieth century migration to industrially developed countries". For analytical convenience, these could be termed the colonial and the post-colonial phases of the Indian diaspora. It is, no doubt, possible to identify overlaps between these two phases: The emigration of Indians that began in the second quarter of the nineteenth century continued into the early decades of the twentieth century. The trickle of emigration of Indians to the "industrially developed countries," which assumed phenomenal proportions in the post-colonial phase, could be noticed in the nineteenth century itself. Nevertheless, it is important to recognize the distinctive nature of these two phases of migration, for their causes, courses and consequences. Studies on Indian diaspora have largely focused on one of the aforementioned phases.

Indian Diaspora in Ancient Times

It should be emphasized, however, that the emigration of Indians has a much longer history than what the reference point of colonialism seems to suggest. In the history of ancient India, we come across accounts of the Buddhist Monks who traveled into remote corners of Central and Eastern Asia. Tinker says Maritime history of pre-colonial India records evidence of continuous contact between the kingdoms of the Coromandel Coast and the islands of South-East Asia. The contact of the Palas of Bengal with the Sailendra kings of Indonesia and the expeditions of the South Indian Cholas which vanquished the great Indonesia Empire of Sri Vijaya are repeatedly referred to by scholars (1977:1).

Vincent Smith (1958) suggests that several elements of Hindu and Buddhist religion, mythology and culture have survived in South-East Asia, and most notably in Thailand and Bali. Tinker says,"Yet none of these contacts led to a distinctive Indian population overseas"(1). The trade with East Africa, however, lead to a permanent Indian settlement there. In the nineteenth century, when "European explorers like Burton first ventured into the interior [in Africa] they were guided on their way by Indian merchants" (2-3). These early migrants to East Africa belonged mainly to small trading communities like the Ismailis, Bhoras and Banyas of the Gujarat region. Their counterparts covering Ceylon, Burma, Malaya, Thailand, and Indonesia were mainly Nattukkottai Chettyars of Chettinad in the Tamil region of South India. Research on the pre-colonial Indian diaspora is scant and sketchy.

Indian Diaspora during European Colonialism

In terms of the magnitude of emigration and its spread, the European colonization, marked by the penetration of mercantile capitalism in Asia, was the most crucial phase in the Indian Diaspora. Large scale emigration of Indians into far off lands was facilitated by the integration of peripheral economies into the emerging world capitalist system, the onset of a revolution in transportation and communication, and the opening of the Suez Canal. The phenomenal trade surpluses earned by the European mercantile class in the wake of geographical discoveries were invested in mines and plantations in Asia, Africa and elsewhere. This created an enormous demand for a cheap and regulated labor force. By the first quarter of the nineteenth century, the demand for labor was accentuated by the ever expanding colonial economy, the growing opposition to slavery and its eventual abolition (by England in 1833, by France in 1848 and by Holland in 1863), and the inability of the European countries to meet the shortfall in labor by deploying their own labor force. A combination of factors made India (and China) an extant reservoir of cheap, docile, and dependable labor, especially to work on the plantations. Tinker (1993) provides one of the most comprehensive surveys of the emigration of Indian labor overseas during the colonial era. Broadly, three distinct patterns of Indian immigration are identified in this period:1) "indentured" labor immigration, 2) kangani and maistry labor immigration, and (3) "passage" or "free" immigration.

The indentured labor immigration, a contract signed by the individual laborer to work on plantations, was officially sponsored by the colonial government. It began in 1834 and ended in 1920. The overwhelming majority of the labor emigrants under this system were recruited from North India. These labor emigrants were taken to the British colonies of British Guiana, Fiji, Trinidad and Jamaica; the French colonies of Guadalupe and Martinique; and the Dutch colony of Surinam. The kangani (derived from Tamil kankani, meaning foreman or overseer) system prevailed in the recruitment of labor for immigration to Ceylon and Malaya (see Jayaraman 1975:6).

Indian Diaspora Writings

Indian Diasporic writings help in many ways and is a powerful network connecting the entire globe. Diasporic literature helps in the circulation of information and in solving many problems too.It helps to re-discover the commonality and inclusiveness of India. This literature works as a channel to strengthen the bonds between the different states of India and of India in relation with the other countries at large.Diasporic opinion helps to break through the past alienation and isolation which caused much injustice and abuse of human rights. It also serves as an outlet to the pent up passions, emotions and feelings, thereby providing a ventilator to grievances and grudges. In other words diasporic literature helps as cathartic indignation. The welfare and wellbeing of the overseas Indians, a sense of security for them and India's greater concern for them is brought out through these writings.

Major Indian Diaspora Writers

Writers of Indian Diaspora are at the centre stage since last decade because of their capturing works. Indian Diaspora occupies second largest place in the world. The population of Diaspora is approximately 25 million, who settled whole notable regions of the world. Indian immigrants in the overseas are for various reasons like free trade, better standards of life and earning. Diasporic or immigrant writing occupies a great place of significance between cultures and countries. Writings Diaspora benefits many ways and a powerful web connects the entire globe. The foremost characteristic features of diaspora writings involve the quest for identity, nostalgia, familial and marital relationships apart from re-rooting, uprooting, multi-cultural milieu etc.

(i) **Bharati Mukherjee**is an Indo American writer and professor at the University of California, Berkeley. She wrote numerous works that cover both fiction and non-fiction. Mukherjee has gone to the extent of contemplating herself as an American writer and not a migrant writer. Her works include novels, short story collections, and one memoir non-fiction. She has won National Book Critics Circle Award in 1988 for '*The Middle and other stories*'. Her other works are

'Jasmine and Wife'. The collection of stories Darkness (1985) focuses the immigrant experience in the USA.

(ii) **Shauna Singh Baldwinis**the Indo-Canadian Diasporic writer. She is the author of two short story collections *'we are not in Pakistan'* and *'English Lessons and other stories'*. The setting of the novel What the Body reminds the partition theme and revolves mainly around three characters Roop, second wife of Sardarji, infertile first wife and Sardarji who life situations. always struggle for his identity. This book bagged Commonwealth Writers Prize for the best book from the region of Caribbean and also long listed for the Orange Prize in fiction.

(iii) **Jhumpa Lahiri**was born to Indian parents from London, who settled in the USA after her birth. Lahiri's debut collection of short stories *'Interpreter of Maladies'* (1999) brought laurels to her by clenching Pulitzer Prize for fiction. In her first novel *'The Namesake'* and her short story collections, she is successful in presenting discontentment at the core in the families she portrays. Her *'Low Land'* is the story of blood relationship that was brutally spoiled by politics, which got shortlisted for the Man Booker Prize.

(iv) **Anjana Appachana** is a novelist of Indian origin who lives in the United States. She has written a book of short stories titled *'Incantations'* and a novel titled *Listening Now* .She is a novelist of Indian origin who lives in the United States. Her debut work *'Incantations and Other Stories'* was first published in England, in the United States and was translated into German language. She is the recipient of O.Henry Festival Prize and National Endowment for the Arts Creative Writing fellowship. Her first novel *'Listening Now'* based on the themes of female bonding, female sexuality and mother-child relations relationships is written in English, but we find nativity in the rhythms of the language and the metaphors.

(v) **Anita Nair**is an EnglishLanguage writer of India. Nair, who hailed from a small village of Kerala was educated in Chennai. Her '*Satyr of the Subway*', a collection of short stories won her a fellowship from Virginia. Nair's novels The Better Man and Ladies Coupe were translated into 21 collections. Her'*Ladies coupe*' is about a middle aged Indian unmarried woman on her journey of self-discovery. The theme of the story is based on a one way train journey which transforms the life and changes the protagonist into a new woman.

(vi) **Chitra Banerjee Divakaruni** isa poet, essayist, author, fiction and short story writer, book reviewer. She is an Indo American poet. Her short story collection *Arranged Marriage and other Stories* brought her the credit of winning the American Book Award in 1995. Her works are largely set in the United States as well as in India. Her focus sometimes is on the experiences of South Asian migrants.

(vii) **ManjulaPadmanabhan**is a playwright, journalist, comic strip artist, an artist, illustrator and cartoonist. She was born in India and grew up in Sweden, Pakistan and Trinidad. Her play *Harvest* was selected for the Onassis Prize in 1997 out of 1470 and bagged the prize. Marginalization and separation are the themes of her writings. Her semi-autobiographical work '*Getting There*' depicts the plight of young woman illustrator in Bombay.

(viii) **Anita Rao Badami** is a writer of South Asia who settled in Canada. Her novels handle with intricacies of Indian family life, cultural gap that is encountered by the immigrants who settle in the west. *The Hero's Walk* was placed on the top five finalists for CBC Canada Reads Competition. The book,'*The Hero's Walk*' describes the problems in the family life and at last how peace evolved into the family.

(ix) **V.S.Naipaul,** aNobel Laureate belongs to Trinidad born in a Hindu Brahmin family. He is a writer of Indian descent, who is popular for pessimistic themes. In the novel *'Area of Darkness'* he focuses on the post-Independence problems like poverty, caste system, neglected areas of sanitation and segregation by society. In *'A House for Mr Biswas'*, Naipaul presents the pathetic state of the protagonist not having a house on his own. His another work, *'TheMimic Men'* criticizes the newly liberated countries and individual's sense of identity.

(x) **Kamala Markandeya** born in Mysore belongs to a Hindu family. She is not only a writer, but a journalist and activist too. Her marriage to the English man, made her settle in London. During intervals, she used to make visits to India. Her ten novels are *'A Silence of Desire'*, *'The Nowhere Man'*, *'The Coffer Dams'*, *'A Handful of Rice'*, *'Possession'*, *'Two Virgins'*, *'The Pleasure city/Shalimar in the American Edition' and 'The Golden Honey Comb'*. Markandeya is ahead of twenty years in predicting the diasporic experiences in her work *'The Nowhere Man'*.

(xi) **Anita Desai** is an Indian writer and professor of Humanities at Massachusetts. Her name was shortlisted for the Booker Prize three times. Desai's novel, *'Fire on the Mountain'* won the Sahitya Academy Award in the year 1978. Her works mainly focus on family in particular, matters about women. Clear light of the day presents the importance of family life. In the work Custody, she describes the problem of alienation of college teacher from his deep rooted culture. Anita is an expert in handling literary technique, the stream of consciousness in the novel Cry the peacock. In another novel *'Bye Bye Black Bird'*, she deals with the problem of adaptability.

(xii) **Salman Rushdie** was born in India and studied at Cambridge in England. He is popularly known for his controversial works. His *'Satanic Verses'* was published amid controversy and violence. It has been banned in various countries. The death sentence was proclaimed against him by the then President ofPakistan. His themes are innovative and about migration and spiritual alienation.

(xiii) **Meera Sayal**was born and brought up in an immigrant Punjabi family in England. Meera Sayal MBEis a British Indian comedian, writer, playwright, singer, journalist and actress. Her Punjabi-born parents came to Britain from New Delhi and she has risen to prominence as one of the most UK's best-known Indian personalities. She was awarded the MBE in the New Year's Honors List in 1997.

(xiv) **Meena Alexander** is an internationally acclaimed poet, writer and scholar. Born in Allahabad, India and brought up in India and Sudan. At present she lives in New York City. She is the author of numerous collections of poetry, essays, and works of fiction, literary memoirs and literary criticism. Her novel *'NampallyRoad'*published in the year 1999 is haunting and lyrical. The novel Nampally*Road* brightly portrays contemporary India a woman's struggle to cut together her past.

(xv) **AmitChaudari**belongs to a new group ofwriters whose roots trace back to the post emergency period in India. Setting in his works is in India and in England. His themes are not revolutionary and turbulent but deals withcity life servants, Indian culture and family life. Themes are close to diasporic experiences. His major works are *'A Strange and sublime Address'* (1991), *'Afternoon Raag'* (1993) *'Freedom Song'* (1998), *'A New World and Real Time' (2002)*

(xvi) **Vikram Seth** became world famous through his novel, *'A Suitable Boy'*. Setting of the novel is in a late post-independent India. The theme of the story is social and financial issues; a Hindu Mother who searches a suitable son in law for her daughter. It highlights the issues like land rights, inter religious marriages and identity crisis in sections. This novel is frequently compared to Leo Tolstoy's *'War and Peace'* by critics and reviewers.

(xvii) **Kiran Desai**is an Indian author. Her novel *'The Inheritance of Loss'* won the 2006 Man Booker Prize and the National Book Critics Circle Fiction Award, is one of the most highly praised Indian writers of second generation. She grew up in India, the U.K. and the U.S.A. where she has settled down. Her debut novel, *'Hullabaloo in the Guava Orchard'* published has praised so much for its subtle portrayal of India. *'The Inheritance of loss'* eclipsed the first novel. This book won the Man Booker Prize in the year 2006 and received The National Book Critics Circle Fiction Award in the year 2007. Themes include post-colonialism and globalization as they relate to a modern India. It is considered a master piece of Indian literature in 21st century.

(xviii)**Sunetra Gupta** is aBengali born writer who is settled in London, has spent her childhood in Ethiopia, Zambia and Liberia. Her debut novel *'Memories of Rain'* published in 1992 won her Sahitya Academy Award in 1996. Her works mainly present stream of consciousness style entering on the interior monologues of the characters.

Diasporic Writing as a Marker of Cultural Identity

The diasporic cultural space is the cultural space that immigrants occupy almost perpetually since assimilation is an ongoing process and no full assimilation ever takes place. Again, as statedabove, it is a space where a contestation is constantly taking place a contestation between the donor culture and the recipient culture. This contest takes place first in the minds of immigrant individuals and Indian DiaporicCommunities and later in their actions. As a result, while trying to make necessary adjustments in this state of contestation between the two contending cultures, diasporic communities or individuals become Janus-faced - looking back, and the gaze fixedstraight ahead. In situations of severe contestation, extreme states of conflict emerge, turning individuals as well as communities into cultural schizophrenics, victims of maladjustment, haunted by, as it were, Hamlet's dilemma-to be or not to be.

Diasporic Writing is rooted in a culture. That is, writers are products of a specificculture, drawing sustenance from it and enriching it in turn. However, the world of diasporic writing belongs to the in-between space we spoke about above, the cultural no-man's land and the site at which cultural armies of a community's past and present clash by day and by night to vanquish each other. Since, it is believed, that creativity lies in the states of fluidity, contest, conflict and instability, diasporicwriters seek this space, locating most oftheir writings here where immigrants are trying to ride two horses simultaneously who more often than not are also pulling them is two different if not opposite directions. The discomfiture and the adventure that results therefrom is what diasporic or immigrant writers relish: from Naipaul to Rushdie, Mistry to Vassanji, immigrantwriters across various locations and times have woven their tapestries from these two-tone yarns and textures.

Conclusion

Diasporic experience is basically about 'home' and 'world' where home stands for the culture of one's origin and world refers to the culture of adoption. Sometimes the concept of home is equated with that of the nation, one is born into and world as the nations one immigrates into or exiles one into. Because of this sense of 'exile', an alternative term used for diasporic experience is 'homelessness', a term that was popularized by Said but that is also a favourite of a writer like V.S.Naipaul. Homi Bhabha would explain this experience in terms of what he calls 'gathering'-"gathering of exiles and emigres and refugees, gathering on the edge of Indian Dasporic Writing'foreign' cultures, gathering at frontiers; gathering in the ghettoes or cafes of city centers" as would he put it. Rushdie, on the other hand, would turn home into 'imaginary homelands' and liken them to broken mirrors some pieces of which are lost irretrievably. However, the picture that emerges out of the broken mirror-that is to say, the diasporic experience-may be different from the one reflected by a mirror that is whole but it is no less significant.

Indian Diasporic writings help in many ways and is a powerful network connecting the entire globe. Diasporic literature helps in the circulation of information and in solving many problems too. It helps to re-discover the commonality and inclusiveness of India. This literature works as a channel to strengthen the bonds between the different states of India and of India in relation with the other countries at large. Diasporic opinion helps to break through the past alienation and isolation which caused much injustice and abuse of human rights. It also serves as an outlet to the pent up passions, emotions and feelings, providing a ventilator to grievances and grudges. In other words diasporie literature helps as cathartic indignation. The welfare and wellbeing of the overseas Indians, a sense of security for them and India's greater concern for them is brought out through these writings.

Works Cited

1. Alexander, M. (n,d.), *The Kenyon Review,* Interview with Meena Alexander.(R.Maxey, Interviewer)

2. Bhabha, Homi.*The Location of Culture*. London:Routledge, 1991.Print.
3. Mukherjee, Bharati.*Darkness*.New Delhi: Penguin India,1999.Print.
4. Mukherjee, Bharati. *Jasmine*. New York:Grove Weidenfield, 1990.Print.
5. Desai, Anita.*Bye Bye Blackbird*. Delhi: Orient Paperbacks, 1985.Print.
6. Desai, Kiran. *The Inheritance of Loss*, New York: Grove Press, 2006. Print.
7. Hugh Tinker, *The Banyan Tree: Overseas Emigrants from India, Pakistan and Bangladesh*. London: OU, 1977. Print.
8. Kumar, J.G. Kumar. *Diasporic Women Writers: As a Social Perspective. IJAHMS Vol 01. No.12, December 2015.*
9. Jain, Ravindra K. *Indian Communities Abroad: Themes and Literature*. New Delhi: Manohar Books. 1993. Print.
10. Jain, R.K and Jasbir (eds.).*Writers of the Indian Diaspora*.Jaipur:Rawat Pub1ications, 1998. Print.
11. Jayaraman.N.*The Indian Diaspora: Dynamics of Migration*. (Etd) New Delhi:Sage Publications,1975.Print.
12. King, B. *V.S.Naipaul*, London: Mac Millan. 1993.Print.
13. Lahiri Jhumpa. *Namesake*, Boston: Houghton Mifflin. 2004.Print.
14. Narang, Harish. "Piya Gaye Rangoon: Inheritance and Ideology in Diaspora Women's Writing." ***Gender and Narrative.*** Rawat Publications:Jaipur2002.Print.
15. Pandey, Abhay. *Indian Diasporic Literature: Creative*, New Delhi. 2008.Print.

• • •

16. Parekh, Bhiku. "Some Reflections on the Indian Diaspora." Journal of Contemporary Thought 3 1993 105-51.Print.
17. *Prbal J. Roddannavar, Themes seen in Diasporic Writings, AJMS, Vol12, Issues3, March 2014, ISSN:2321-8819.*
18. Vincent A. Smith: *The Oxford history of India. Third edition, edited by Percival Spear*. xv, 898 pp., 40 plates, map. Oxford: Clarendon Press, 1958. 42*s*.

CONTRIBUTION OF INDIAN DIASPORA TO THE DEVELOPMENT OF INDIA: AN OVERVIEW

Dr. G. Jeya Jeevakani
Assistant Professor of English
Thiagarajar College of Engineering
Madurai – 15.

Diasporas are transnational communities formed by emigration including the forced emigration. The concept of Diaspora is not a new idea as it was mentioned in the classical period. The term is applied to many groups including Armenian, Chinese, Greeks, Kurds, Tamils, etc. The main idea is the dispersal from an original homeland memory and myth about the homeland and maintenance of boundary. Diaspora has become a trendy term and concept in the modern world. Most of the countries become multicultural, multiethnic, multiracial and pluralistic due to Diasporas. These immigrants and emigrants are referred as refugees, asylum seekers, guest workers once. These communal contenders are under the single rubric of Diaspora nowadays. In the view of Vijay Mishra, Diaspora is a product of fantasy, "a joy, a pleasure around which anti-miscegenation narratives of homeland are constructed" (Vijay Mishra, "The Diasporic Imaginary: Theorizing the Indian Diaspora," Textual Practice 10: 1 (Spring 1996,422-423.))

The term Diaspora is from the Greek word "diasperien" means scatter seeds across (Wikipedia – the free Encyclopedia). The basic of this term is from the Hebrew word "galut" means exile from the Holy land (The new Encyclopedia of Britannica (vol.3)). Diaspora is used by the

Greek to refer to the citizens of a grand city, who migrated to the conquered land. And it also refers the dispersal of Jews from Palestine all over the world. This term carries religious, physical, philosophical and eschatological connotations. So, the term Diaspora is used to refer any man/woman of various ethnicisms forced to leave his/ her homelands; scattered all over the world; and started developments in his/her dispersal and culture. Today Diaspora brings many range of ethnic communities, variety of categories such as political and war refugees, migrants, immigrants, transnational communities, etc. together.

Leaving the mother country and going abroad such as the USA, the UK, and Canada is not a simple move one makes. It is a life changing experience because they leave behind everything; the friends, the family members, society, personal identity, to search for better future. If a person goes abroad, his / her life will improve and settle with prosperity is a commonly understood perception. But the reality is different; the NRI faces many hardships. The challenges of Diaspora are very real and very difficult to achieve a higher place. Despite the hardships they face in day to day life, they try to help the homeland.

Indian Diaspora contributes much for the development of India in all levels like social, economical and political. Indian Diaspora acts like a bridge between the host and the home, and it helps to build a good relationship with other countries. Indian Diaspora helps to spread this heritage all the world. Indian Diasporas contribute greater to the economic development of India. Though they are in various forums, workplace and institution basically, they play a crucial role. Indian Diasporas are ready to preserve Indian ethnicism, rights and so on. The late External affairs minister Sushma Swaraj said that, "Indian Diaspora's contribution towards

India is on the rise and so is its importance. Migration of the educated has brought laurels to India."

The following Diaspora Indians have gone places and brought great glory to the country they were born. From science to arts, business to literature, here is a list of exceptionally talented Non Resident Indians (NRIs) who have given the country several more reasons to be proud of:

1. **Rohinton Mistry-** This internationally acclaimed writer was born in Mumbai and did his BA from St. Xavier's College, Mumbai. He later shifted to Canada in 1975 with his wife. He published his first book, 11 connected short stories titled Swimming Lessons and Other Stories from the Firozsha Bag in 1987. His second book *Such a Long Journey,* was published in 1991 and achieved huge national and international acclaim.
2. **Anita Desai and Kiran Desai-** This mother-daughter duo is famous for exceptional writing skills. Kiran Desai's novel The Inheritance of Loss won the Man Booker Prize in 2006 and the National Book Critics Circle Fiction Award. The exceptional writing comes as an inheritance, as Kiran's mother Anita Desai has also been short-listed for the Booker Prize thrice. Kiran has been winning accolades from various notable figures ever since she published her first book. Anita won the **Sahitya Award Academy** in 1978 for her novel Fire on the Mountain and has also won the British Guardian Prize for The Village by the Sea. Anita is a Fellow of the Royal Society of Literature, the American Academy of Arts and Letters and also writes for the New York Review of Books. Her novel In Custody is one of her finest works.
3. **Bharati Mukherjee** is an Indo American writer and professor at the University of California, Berkeley. She wrote numerous works that cover both fiction and non-

fiction. Mukherjee has gone to the extent of contemplating herself as an American writer and not a migrant writer. Her works include novels, short story collections, and one memoir non-fiction. She has won National Book Critics Circle Award in 1988 for 'The Middle and other stories'. Her other works are 'Jasmine and Wife'. The collection of stories 'Darkness' (1985) focusses the immigrant experience in the USA.

4. **Shauna Singh Baldwin** is the Indo-Canadian Diasporic writer. She is the author of two short story collections 'We are not in Pakistan' and 'English Lessons and other stories'. Her stories in the short story collections have been published in various literary magazines.
5. **Jhumpa Lahiri** was born to Indian parents from London, who settled in the USA after her birth. Lahiri's debut collection of short stories 'Interpreter of Maladies' (1999) brought laurels to her by clenching Pulitzer Prize for fiction. In her first novel 'The Namesake' and her short story collections, she is successful in presenting discontentment at the core in the families she portrays. Her 'Low Land' is the story of blood relationship that was brutally spoiled by politics, which got shortlisted for the Man Booker Prize.
6. **Anjana Appachana** is a novelist of Indian origin who lives in the United States. She has written a book of short stories titled 'Incantations' and a novel titled 'Listening Now'. Her debut work 'Incantations and Other Stories' was first published in England, in United States and was translated into German language. Anjana Appachana is the recipient of O.Henry Festival Prize and National Endowment for the Arts Creative Writing fellowship.
7. **Chitra Banerjee Divakaruni** is poet, essayist, author, fiction and short story writer, book reviewer. She is an

Indo American poet. Her short story collection Arranged Marriage and other Stories brought her the credit of winning the American Book Award in 1995. Her works are largely set in the United States as well as in India. Her focus sometimes is on the experiences of South Asian migrants.

8. **Manjula Padmanabhan** is a playwright, journalist, comic strip artist, an artist, illustrator and cartoonist. She was born in India and grew up in Sweden, Pakistan and Trinidad. Her play Harvest was selected for the Onassis Prize in 1997 out of 1470 and bagged the prize. Marginalization and separation are the themes of her writings. Her semi-autobiographical work 'Getting There' depicts the plight of young woman illustrator in Bombay.
9. **V.S.Naipaul** a Nobel Laureate belongs to Trinidad born in a Hindu Brahmin family. Writer of Indian descent, popular for pessimistic themes. In the novel 'Area of Darkness' he focusses on the post-Independence problems like poverty, caste system, neglected areas of sanitation and segregation by society. In 'A House for Mr Biswas', Naipaul presents the sorry state of protagonist having house on his own. 'The Mimic Men' criticises the newly liberated countries and individual's sense of identity.
10. **Kamala Markandeya** was born in Mysore belongs to a Hindu family. She is not only a writer but journalist and activist too. Her marriage to English man, made her settle in London. During intervals, she used to make visits to India. Her novel 'Nectar in a Sieve' is translated into more than dozen languages with the theme, the pathetic plight of a poor peasant. Markandeya is ahead of twenty years in predicting the diasporic experiences in her work 'The Nowhere Man'.

11. **Salman Rushdie** was born in India and studied at Cambridge in England. He is popularly known for his controversial works. His 'Satanic Verses' was published amid controversy and violence. It has been banned in various countries. Death sentence was proclaimed against him by the then President of Pakistan. His themes are innovative and about migration and spiritual alienation.
12. **Amit Chaudari** belongs to a new group of writers whose roots trace back to the post emergency period in India. Setting in his works is in India and in England. His themes are close to diasporic experiences and deal with city life servants, Indian culture and family life. His major works are 'A Strange and sublime Address' (1991), 'Afternoon Raag' (1993) 'Freedom Song' (1998), 'A New World and Real Time' (2002)
13. **Vikram Seth** became world famous through his novel 'A Suitable Boy'. Setting of the novel is in a late post-independent India. The theme of the story is social and financial issues. It highlights the issues like land rights, inter religious marriages and identity crisis in sections. This novel is frequently compared to Leo Tolstoy's 'War and Peace' by critics and reviewers.

The list of diaspora writers are too lengthy to mention. The experiences and sufferings reflected in the literature they produced in the midst of many issues and problems and they bring laurels to the mother nation.

The Indian Diasporas show interest in the activities happening in India. The NRI and PIOs, support both with money and manpower. The government considers diaspora as an asset. Ram Madhav, the General Secretary of BJP once said, "Indian Diaspora can be India's voice even while being loyal citizens in those countries. That is the long term goal behind the Diaspora diplomacy. It is the way the Jewish community looks out for Israel's interests in the United States." So, the government of India started "The High Level Committee on Indian Diaspora (HLC)", on 18th August, 2000. This committee had some important tasks that are listed below:

- Study the characteristics, aspirations, attitudes, requirements, strengths and weaknesses of the Indian diaspora and their expectations from India
- Study the role that the PIOs and NRIs may play in the economic, social and technological development of India
- Recommend a broad but flexible policy framework and country-specific plans for forging a mutually beneficial relationship with PIOs and NRIs and for facilitating their participation in India's economic development.

The HLC identified that twenty million Diasporas spread over 134 countries. And this committee celebrated the success of Indian Diaspora who helped to change the opinion of the world in getting favour from other countries. So, the Indian Government had a vision of connecting more with its Diasporas across the world, and succeeded in its vision by organizing 15th Pravas Bharatiya Diwas (PBW) on 21st to 23rd January 2019. This was the first time the Indian Government awarded and encouraged the Indian origin eminent personalities across the world. This is to connect with the homeland and at the same time maintain and progress the richness of India in a foreign soil. As a result of this, India's engagement with people of Indian origins has taken on many different forms and occupies so many different spheres. These forms range from levels of personal family ties to business ventures involving international financial markets.

The Government started persuading Diasporas through words: 1. "When you left this country, you carried with you the primary colours of the Indian ethos. A cross-fertilisation of cultures over time has added new shades to those vibrant hues. Today we invite you to brush in some of these new colours onto the ever-evolving canvas of India's development." 2. "The government wanted the riches of the Diaspora but used an emblematic language to articulate and tone down its primary intent: 'We do not want only your investments. We also want your ideas. We do not want your riches, we want the richness of your experiences'. This veneer of the poetic Vajpayee continued even under the administration of the rather impassive Prime Minister Manmohan Singh: 'I would like you to reach out and invest in a new India. Invest not just financially, but intellectually, socially, culturally and, above all, emotionally'".

The population of the diaspora gradually increased and this becomes the essential factor in international politics. The Indian Diasporas have so many elements for their success. They were "model Minority, now the number is growing constantly. Many engaged in politics, multinational business and so on. This makes India to reach its potential fast. Indian benefitted much of Indian Diaspora. The government's foreign policy shows the outreach to the Indian Diaspora. India has not only benefits but also problems like negative campaigning, separatist movements, etc.. create a lots of problems in India. They become the sensitive issues and affect the security system of the country.

The government of India aims and have a strategy to have partnership with Diaspora to complete the projects like Swachh Bharat, Clean Ganga, Digital India. The Indian Diasporas have plenty of opportunities to contribute to the homeland and to raise the Indian society sufficiently, and act as Indian 'ambassadors' and prove their potential. This provides a great strength to the Nation.

Work Cited

1. Mishra, Vijay "The Diasporic Imaginary: Theorizing the Indian Diaspora." *Textual Practice* 10: 1 Spring 1996: 422-423.
2. www.orfonline.org
   https://www.thebetterindia.com › 14725 › famous-nri-famous-nri-non-resident-indian-..
   http://publications.anveshanaindia.com

EXPLORING THE INTERSTITIAL SPACES IN JHUMPA LAHIRI'S '*HELL-HEAVEN*'

Mohanan P
Research Scholar,
Jamal Muhammed College, Trichy, Bharathidasan University
mohanputhi@rediffmail.com

Dr. Abdul Mohammed Ali Jinnah
Associate Proffessor,
Jamal Muhammed College, Trichy
Bharathidasan University

Introduction

This paper is an attempt to examine the interstitial spaces in the story *Hell-Heaven* written by Jhumpa Lahiri, the new generation diaspora writer. The story is a mirror onto the problems of identity crisis and cross-cultural consciousness. The story provides a number of spaces where the reader can read against the grain and construct meanings out of the unwritten text. Lahiri speaks of the metaphorical spaces of Hell and Heaven that stand for inner experiences of the characters. There are a number of instances in the story that permits a striking interaction of varied spatial relations which can be explored in the light of the events, people, their relationships with one another and the complexities they live with. Everyone is an outsider in an inner world of myriad experiences. An exploration into the regions of the inner self can fruitfully explain the mysteries of individuals and their actions. The writer also tries to establish the concept that the meaning of a text lies not in the words written, but the spaces it provides to the reader to explore for further interpretations and meaning making. A critical reading is possible only when the reader engages in the acts of delving deep into the spaces to gleanthe gems of abstractions.

The themes of Jhumpa Lahiri's story 'Hell-Heaven', similar to the themes of most of the diaspora writers, are cultural alienation, identity crisis, cross-cultural consciousness, etc. 'Diasporic literature generally deals with alienation, existential rootlessness, nostalgia and identity crisis and quest for identity. It also deals with issues related to the disintegration of cultures.' (Dr.T.RajaSekhar 2016). Jhumpa Lahiri's works usually reflect the life of the Bengali immigrants in India. 'Hell-Heaven' mainly discusses the problems related to love and marriage. The story is a quintessence of diasporic literature as it deals with the traumas of disillusion, cultural ambivalence, and the confusions brought about by the cultural shock.

The 'Hell' and 'Heaven' in the story are the interior spaces of sense regions. There are a number of instances in the story that permits a striking interaction of varied spatial relations. The interstitial spaces in the story can be explored in the light of the interior perceptions of the characters and the complexities and complications they experience both 'inside' and 'outside.'

Jhumpa Lahiri as a Diaspora Writer

The term 'diaspora' is derived from the Greek word 'Diaspeirein' which means 'to scatter about, to disperse.' The preposition 'Dia' means 'over' and the word 'speirein' means 'to sow or to scatter'. The word today is widely used in the sense of a large number of people, generally belonging to the same group, moving from their homeland and settling in an alien land. According to Walter Connor, diaspora refers to the 'segment of people living outside the homeland' (Connor

1991: 83). In a wider sense, diaspora implies any population dispersed in space. 'The term that once described Jewish, Greek and Armenian dispersion now shares meanings with a larger semantic domain that includes words like immigrant, expatriate, refugee, guest worker, exile community, overseas community, ethnic community.' (Tololyan 1991 p.4)

Stuart Hall defines diaspora not as "the scattered tribes whose identity can only be secured in relation to some sacred homeland to which they must at all costs return…" He defines diaspora experience "not by essence or purity, but by the recognition of a necessary heterogeneity and diversity; but by a conception of 'identity' which lives with and through, not despite, difference; by *hybridity*." M.R Chandran and T. Senthamarai observe, "The immigrants have been ruptured with the loss of sense of belongingness, neither to their homeland nor in the land of immigration. They have been haunted consequently with a number of mounting problems like alienation, displacement, isolation, discrimination, cultural conflicts, nostalgia for the homeland, barrier in communication which are the ingredients of the painful life of the immigrants." Jhumpa Lahiri's characters display the conflicts, angst, confusion, clashes and despair ensued by the inevitable plight of estrangement similar to the ones the immigrants are exposed to and her works reflect the dual worlds where the characters experience an inexpressible trauma irresistibly manifested by the detachment from their homeland and native culture.

Diaspora suggests not merely the scattering, but also "the anticipation of root-taking and eventual growth" and also "a sense of tenacity, resistance, and preservation of faith during the worst circumstances." (Nico Israel 2000) Amit Shankar Saha speaks about the advantages of living as a migrant, such as 'the privilege of having a double perspective, of being able to experience diverse cultural mores, of getting the leverage provided by the networking within the Diasporic community, and more.' The 'pride, honour and prosperity' that the immigrants develop as an essential positivity engendered by their struggles to sustain and survive in an alien culture for securing stability and settlement help them blend in with the culture of their homeland and the culture of the new land. Usha, in *Hell-Heaven*, is a second generation immigrant who adapts easily to the environment and even passionately yearns for following the new ways of living forgetting her parents' cultural heritage. For Lahiri, India was not her homeland, as she herself admits in an interview with Vibhuti Patel, in Newsweek International, "I didn't grow up there. I wasn't a part of things. We visited often, but we didn't have a home. We were clutching with a world that was never fully with us." It was perhaps this hydroponic root which could not cling to anywhere that made her portray her new generation characters with the same ambivalent attitude.

Jhumpa Lahiri is a diaspora writer in the sense that she translates her own thoughts, feelings and experiences as an immigrant into lores of cultural diversity and the identity crisis replicating the salient issues of diaspora ranging from the loss of the sense of the belonging to the total despair and sense of alienation. Usha's parents in the story *Hell-Heaven*, who represent the first generation immigrant, face such a dilemma and a feeling of being uprooted, and they strenuously struggle to adapt themselves to the alien culture, trying hard to imitate the new culture and to negotiate, although in vain. But the second generation immigrants, as represented by Usha, easily identify and blend in. *Hell-Heaven* is an attempt to investigate into the chaos and complexities of a dislocated family and the psychological nature of the disrupted generations whose predicament is to live in "two worlds" of troubled legacies.

Interstitial Spaces in *Hell-Heaven*

Jennifer Anna Gosetti-Ferencei defines 'interstitial spaces' as "broadly indicating not merely the intervening spaces between fixed empirical or geometrical points, but space constituted by striking negotiations of the relation between different positions with experiences or between different forms of experience. These interstitial spaces are not measurable by empirical means and must be achieved through poetic efforts. It might denote the space between the self and the world, between words and thoughts, between the past and present, between the real and the imagined, between the native culture and the alien culture, and between the inter-phenominal "regions" of different senses, generally created by a keen response to the crises of spaces of physical and psychological manifestations. It is, in fact, these spaces, not the written words, that communicate more eloquently, as it provides the reader with the privilege of exploring these spaces to construct meanings.

According to Roland Barthes, "a text is not a line of words releasing a single 'theological meaning' (the message of the author God) but a multidimensional space in a variety of writings, none of them original, blend and clash. The text is a tissue of quotations drawn from the innumerable centers of culture." (The Death of the Author 1977). He also argues, "The text is plural. Which is not simply to say that it has several meanings, but that it accomplishes the very plural of meanings: an irreducible (and not merely an acceptable) plural. The text is not a co-existence of meanings, but a passage, an overcrossing; thus it answers not to an interpretation, even a liberal one, but to an explosion, a dissemination". ('From Work to Text', proposition 4, 1971) A text can be considered as a woven material of ideas, the meanings of which often lie, not in the words, but in the interstitial spaces that each word, sentence or the discourse as whole permits. The very responsibility of the reader is not to interpret the text but to 'read against the grains' and explore what is not said.

The interstitial nature of places, people, actions and emotions are very much evidenced in the story *Hell-Heaven*. The daughter and mother, the husband and wife, the host and guest, all find themselves in-between. Each one tries to resist the arbitrary and superimposed spaces created by cultural dilemma, which is juxtaposed to their willed acceptance of their predicament and willing congeniality to the newly created environments. The protagonist, Usha, lives in a rented apartment in Central Square with his parents, Shyamal and Aparna. This apartment is an 'interstitial space' on a number of levels. In a sense, it constrains and produces identity. It is here that we see both the hell and the heaven that make the life of the inmates as well as Pranab convoluted. The apartment here creates a metaphoric space that safeguards the inmates against the outsiders in one instance, and that creates prisons for those who are inside. It stands for asDr. Anil S. Sugate observes that hell is the situation of the narrator's mother. Her monotonous life suddenly becomes a heaven when she meets Pranab, who later creates hell for everyone, including his wife.

Pranab is a direct contrast to Shyamal in many aspects. Both are first generation immigrants, but differ in their outlook towards life and culture. Initially, Pranab finds it very hard to adapt to the new ways of life in America. His hardships make him think of packing his bed and leave. The situation was a hell for him. But he found Usha's house a heaven, where he could sense identical tastes and views, and above all, a connection with his own culture. Pranab calls Shyamal 'Da' which means elder brother and Aparna, 'Boudi' which means sister-in-law. Usha's mother loved his presence, and they both shared a lot of things together. They liked each other's company. Usha narrates,"...Pranab Kaku's visits were what my mother looked forward to all day, that she changed into a new sari and combed her hair in anticipation of his arrival, and that she planned, days in advance, the snacks she would serve him with such nonchalance." (*Hell-Heaven*). The apartment is the space where the conservative mother realizes the reality that her daughter is distancing herself with her roots. The mother finally accepts the situation and becomes prepared to negotiate identities. Usha says, " My mother and I had also made peace; she had accepted the fact that I was not only her daughter but a child of America as well".The apartment thus stands as an intermediate space between two cultures. AS Rushdie says, "We are at one and the same time insiders and outsiders in this society." Usha's mother is both an insider and outsider in her own realms. The hell and heaven are metaphoric interiors. Life once again becomes a hell for her when Pranab decides to marry Deborah, an American girl. She even makes an attempt to suicide. She believes that Pranab has changed completely because of Deborah's influence, She says , " He used to be different. I don't understand how a person can change so suddenly. It's just hell-heaven."Later we see that her anticipations about Pranab come true. He marries a married Bengali woman and destroys two families. Here he goes back to his cultural ties in an attempt to find heaven in his roots. He was destroying himself by accepting the new identity. Heaven and hell are metaphoric spaces parallel to the inner spaces of the characters and represent sense experiences.

•••

There can be seen a striking interaction of all spaces in the story- the textual, metaphoric, descriptive and narrative spaces converge to suggest new meanings. The descriptive spaces of the domestic scenes where members of the family live as separate entities, but communicating between their interior and exterior spaces become part of the narrative spaces. Usha's mother, a self-centred woman, alienates everyone around her. Her relationship with her husband is not a satisfactory one. Shyamal is a workaholic man for whom his work is heaven. She is neurotic, but as a desperate woman cast into a world of lost identities, she deserves sympathy. Coleman observes, "Usually the neurotic vaguely senses that something is missing, that she is not fulfilling herself or leading a truly meaningful life. And this, in turn, leads to feelings of futility and unhappiness, to a 'loss of joy'". Her hostile relationship with Usha makes her paranoiac that Usha might marry an American. She refuses to allow Usha to wear a bra. This desperate woman, who has never been placated by her husband, becomes lonely and disgusted with mundane life. Even her only child started defying her. According to Dibyadyuti Roy, Aparna represents "the liminality of female postcolonial bodies everywhere and constantly negotiates patriarchy, and imperialism alongside the troubling legacies of mother(land), diaspora and belonging." She is a victim of the male dominated spaces that bring in excruciating sufferings to her.

While exploring the textual space, one may come across the stories within the story. The feelings and preoccupations of each character spawn the consequent trauma and agony. Each character expresses a metaphoric view of the world different from one another. Most often these views fail to consolidate the personal and socio-cultural anticipations, and being unreal they engage in a conflict and subsequent struggles with the self. It affects the diasporic familial relationships. Thus the theme of the story is a journey "across visible and invisible frontiers that the characters must transgress in order to find their real self." (Anca Dobrinescu-2000). The conflict is engendered mainly by the 'encounter between the self and the other', and between the perceptions of the external world and the inner space, which thereby create a confused inner world. Spatial relations transform into the spatiality of the inner consciousness and promote a communion between the interior and the exterior spaces. Both the first and second generation characters in the story are seen invariably struggle in finding their sense of location.

Hell-Heaven is a story of two triangular relations. The first triangle is formed by Shyamal, Aparna and Pranab and the second by Pranab, Deborah and the Bengali woman Pranab marries. Usha, the narrator, occupies a position, neither in nor out of these triangles. She attempts to maintain a tie with both the triangles, but utterly fail. The intermediate zone she accepts is more convenient to her, because she is struggling between the parental legacy and the new enchanting culture of America. Here, the hell is Usha, as she moves away from her culture and traditions to embrace the American culture and creates an insurmountable space between herself and her family. Aparna is shocked at first to notice her daughter's growing affiliation towards the American culture, but later she is forced to accept her as she is a woman who is afraid of change. She passively accepts her destiny and fails to initiate resolutions or influence the other people around her.

It is paradoxical that Debora is an outsider in her own country as she never was able to understand the language, culture, food and history of her husband and she failed to assert her identity in the family. She remarks to Aparna, "I was so horribly jealous of you back then, for knowing him, understanding him in a way I never could." (p.83). The detached space between herself and Pranab remained live for twenty three years till finally they got estranged. Throughout the story Aparna considered Deborah an outsider, because of her jealousy. Debora, on the other hand develops jealousy towards Aparna for maintaining a cultural intimacy with her husband.Though Deborah is a stereotypical American in her appearance and behaviour, she distances herself from both her culture and the Indian culture and places herself in a space between the two.

Conclusion

Jhumpa Lahiri, through her deceptively translucent narrative style, fruitfully illustrates the interstitial spaces in the story Hell-Heaven and allows the reader to make an attempt to explore the deeper senses that facilitates better understanding and critical evaluation of the text. The interaction of the various spaces constitutes the totality of the text. The peripheral meaning of a text can contribute only the minimum appreciation, whereas an inquisition into the meanings created by the interactive and conspicuous spaces can contribute to the understanding of the text to the optimal levels.Viewing through the cultural lens, we can see that *Hell-Heaven* is a piece of diasporic literature that juxtaposes the two distinct cultures from which emanate the struggles for negotiating the alien culture. To a great extent, the first generation diaspora can imitate the new culture. But the second generation, being brought up in the new cultural setting, adapt with and rather adopt the culture of their second home. Jhumpa Lahiri tries to equate the politics of identity with the politics of spaces and contribute enormously to the diasporic conjectures of conflicting displacement.

Works Cited

1. Hall, Stuart. "*Cltural Identity and Diaspora*", in Jonathan Rutherford ed. *Identity: Community, Culture , Difference*. London : Lawrence &Wishart 1990; 222-37.
2. Brubaker, Rogers. The 'diaspora' diaspora, Ethnic and Racial Studies Vol. 28 No. 1 January 2005 pp. 1- 19.
3. M.R.Chandran and T. Senthamari. Female Diasporic Sensitivities in Jhumpa Lahiri's Unaccustomed Earth, Internatinal Journal of English, Language, Literature and Translation, Vol.3, issue 3, 2016.
4. Dityadyuti Ray. Illicit Motherhood: Recrafting Post Colonial Feminist Resistance in Edna O' Brien's 'The Love Object' and Jhumpa Lahiri's 'Hell-Heaven'.
5. Israel, Nico. *'Outlandish: Writing Between Exile and Diaspora'*. StanfordUniversity Press, 2000
6. Mishra, Vijay. The Literature of the Indian Diaspora: Theorizing the Diasporic Imaginary, Postcolonial Text, Vol 4, No 2 (2008), Routledge, London.
7. Monaco, Angelo. Jhumpa Lahiri, the Interpreter of the New Indian Diaspora,Impossibilia No9, páginas 72-92 (Abril 2015) ISSN 2174-2464.
8. Dr. Sugate, Anil S. 'Home, Hybridity and Love: Diasporic Relocations in Jhumpa Lahiri's Hell-Heaven
9. Dr. T. Raja Sekhar. *'Indian Diaspora and Its Development: A Brief Study'* in Research Journal of English Language and Literature, Vol.4, Issue 4, 2016 (Oct-Dec) ISSN 2395-2636

OVERCOMING LIMINALITIES THROUGH MULTICULTURALISM: A REFLECTION IN INDIAN WOMEN'S DIASPORIC WRITING

Dr. G. Karthiagiselvi M.A.,M.Phil.,Ph.D.
Assistant Professor of English
Saraswathi Narayanan College, Madurai

Introduction:

This paper deals with the reflection of multiculturalism in diasporic writing and the way the diaspora writers deals with these aspects to overcome their liminalities. In addition, it explores the concept of culture, identity and the process of identity formation among immigrants. Liminalities can be overcome by assimilating the cultural changes. Slowly people are adjusting to the changing norms of American society. Tradition is thus a flexible and dynamic concept which allows communities a link between the past and the present, and helps them to sustain their culture. Instead of placing themselves in one culture, they have chosen a two - tiered culture and maintain an umbilical link with the past and the present values systems. This duality arises out of necessity, and not by choice. The characters through a process of transplantation pull themselves out of the liminalities and replant themselves in the multicultural scenario.

Cross - cultural confrontation has received a maximum impetus since the emergency of the modernist movement in the beginning of the 20th century. The Globalization of World economy can be looked upon as a natural offshoot of multiculturalism and intercultural interaction. Every culture has its own peculiarities and predilections which evokes a mixed response in one form or another in different cultural aspects. People quite often try their best to forge a workable synthesis between their native cultural and that of the new set - up. This process is not a smooth one and results in some psychological eccentricities alien to both the cultures.

Culture is too vast and baffling a term to be precisely defined. Culture is that which makes life worth living. Thus culture is a quest for good but it is not good if the quest is not a free choice. The quest and choice are the two ingredients of culture and the tradition is formed by the culmination of history or a tradition may be defined as a passage in which there is both persistence and renewal. So, quest and culture are both ancient and contemporary, traditional as well as modern .

Eliot believes that there is a very close relationship between culture and religion. It is religion of people which makes them have something in common but their differences might bring a clash among their followers. Eliot regards culture of people as an incarnation of its religion for want of a better term to avoid misconception by the communities creates social, culture and linguistic confusion and this becomes a great hurdle in the formation of a national culture and as time passes, the old values gradually diminish leaving their remnants in their memories while the migration in modern times is entirely otherwise.

The class which moves out of its cultural contours,have no love lost for its culture. Instead there is so much of cultural mixing in the post –colonial era that it has given birth to hybrid –culture post colonial culture is inevitably a hybrid phenomenon involving a dialectical relationship between the grafted European culture system and as an indigenous ontology within its impulse to create or recreate an independent local identity such construction or reconstruction occurs as a dynamic interaction between Europeanhegemony and peripheral subversions of them Ashcroft and his colleagues.

The immigrants moving between the two poles of nationalism and Westernization has given birth to the idea of multiculturalism resulting in the upsurge hybrid culturalism. With this situation, there came a galaxy of writers who constructed the history of past and present including geographical shift of location, cultural dilemma, and modification in the nature of personal relationship, suffocation emerging out of language barrier and the lack of adaptability. This collective phenomenon of cultural migration drastically mingled with the issues of gender binaries and racial prejudices. These aspects awakened the consciousness of the host of the writers representing the twilight view of the life and these writers have collectively been called as 'Diasporic Writers'.

The word 'diaspora' is derived from the Greek ' dia' (through) and ' sperien' (scatter). According to Webster's dictionary, diaspora refers to 'dispersion', and so the word embodies a notion of a center, a 'home' journey. We can interpret both the concepts – as a spread of population and a forcible dispersal. Diasporic journeys are essentially about settling down, about having roots elsewhere. Presently the meaning of diaspora may be limited to any sizeable community of a particular nation outside its own country, sharing same common attachments that gives an identity to that social group . People have been migrating since evolution, in search of better living. The process of migration is a continuous one, only thing is boundaries my change, some national some may be across the nations. The migrants not only take their skills and expertise, but also their culture, modes of life and ideologies to their destination. They can influence the demographic, economic and social structure to create a new culture identity. These aspects of diasporic communities enter into literature. The diasporic writers have inevitably produce works of lecture comprising of their history and heritage, highlighting their problems, its achievement, limitation, challenges and frustration. The diasporic themes and issues can best be studied through a multidisciplinary approach.

The category called 'Indian diaspora' has been used in this article. Much of the diasporic literature that gets published and gains attention is written in English. Usually, Asian Indian literature in English is prominently featured across the world both in the academic and on the internet. South Asian diaspora is strewn with the names of Indian writers from V.S.Naipaul to Bharathi Mkherjee, Chitra Banerjee and to more recent Jhumpa Lahiri. Literature is an important tool for maintaining ethnic identity. It is an ethnic symbol, which distinguishes one group of diaspora from the other. This paper typically deals with Indian diaspora in America is it opens up several themes and many relevant issues which helps us to understand multi cultural experience from the point of view of America and that of diasporic Indian there. Most of the Women Indian diasporic writers write neither to fight male domination nor to compromise themselves but they portray the reality of what we call – femaleness, marriage, sex, children, culture and socially acceptable position of being a woman. The works of all the women diaspora deals with the concept of cultural transplantation and each migrant has his or her own story to tell. All the protangonists of the literary works crave for identity and identity depends on the sense of displacement, loss of home, nostalgia, culture, ethnic consciousness, religion, caste groups, language etc.

Of the galaxy of Indian Women diasporic writing, we normally come across the names of Bharathi Mukherjee, Chitra Banerjee and Jhumpa Lahiri. The above three women writers represent the faces of transition in diasporic literature. Bharathi Mukherjee being the oldest mainly concentrates on Expatriate Nostalgia whereas Chitra Banerjee deals with immigration and acculturation. More recently, Jhumpa Lahiri – the youngest of all the above three mainly writes about the insights in the diversity of response of the three generation of immigrants. The first generations of immigrants suffer the trauma of alienation. The 2nd generations of immigrants promote the aesthetics of 'acceptance', reaffirmation and assimilation. However the third generation i.e the children of immigrants are free from the burden of divided consciousness but they inculcate the psyche of an 'aloof' self in homeland and host land. The children of immigrants inspite of being born native cannot fully segregate themselves from their ancestral cultural heritage and subsequently bloom to inspire them to reclaim their native cultural identity. Mrs. Divakaruni writes with the assumptions that inspite of the opulence of the West, Indian immigrants constantly re-define and re-shape the conditions of their tied with the uncompromising bonds of personal relationship.

The short stories in *Arranged Marriage* are beautifully narrated stories of lives which are transformed or trapped by cultural changes, all the women protagonists struggle fiercely to carve out an identity of their own. In the stories of *Arranged Marriage,* Divakaruni constructs the consciousness of Indian couples seeking shelter in American society with their uncompromising bonding with their national identity, craving for personal relationship, their desperate urge to redefine the man-women relationship in than-cultural spaces. The elements of spiritualism, money and technology are interwoven which compromises the texture of stories in arranged Marriage. Divakaruni has used these stories to represent the reality of the shifting paradigms of social spectacle. Her literature reflects the exiting patterns of thoughts, feeling and actions of the contemporary society.

The very first story in this collection entitled 'Bats' is written in the self-revelation style where the narrator expresses her curiosity to unveil the secret of personal life of her parents. Her consciousness is gripped with the unrevealed sobbing of her mother. In the recollections of her past she reminds of the pure joy that she had experienced in the company of her grandparents. She recalls the joy of the beauty of nature and the excitement of fun the fish pond. In this story, the diasporic consciousness has been subordinated to the issue that the friction between parents creates greater chaos and uncertainty in the life of children.

In the story 'Clothes' the writer portrays the life of Sumita who is married to Somesh. The author reflects the two images of Sumita. On the one hand she is depicted happy to marry an NRI but on the other hand she is portrayed as a confused woman. After her marriage she tries hand to satisfy her husband in every possible way. Just like all other Indian wives she performs all the household services needed by her husband, whose satisfaction is her pleasure in life. Somesh works out in a store which is open round the clock. This heavy workload doesn't allow the newlymarried couple to spend time together. They longed to be together which turned out to be impossible. Many a time, she feels thrown away into an alien world but makes an effort to withstand the impact of western culture and tradition. Towards the end tragedy dooms on her when Somesh gets killed by burglars. Sumita's life is shattered but she doesn't lose her courage. She gets ready to face the future with a strong mind. When Somesh is killed in the sore, friends perform all the rituals. Thus, it is clear that Indian custom and traditions are still maintained in a fast paced land, America. Sumita doesn't wish to stay in the home like most other Indian widows. She envisions herself dressed in the clothes her husband gets her and imagines working in the store.

Therefore the story points out that American culture is not always viewed from a negative perspective. It can also transform the superstitious Indian culture into a rational one.

The story 'Silver Pavement and Golden Roofs' is a sentimental account of the twilight of 'home' and 'homelessness'. The idea of cultural confrontation and the complexity of man- woman relationship are synthesized. Jayanti, a young migrant from India lives with her uncle. She starts making a comparative evaluation of her life at Calcutta and the horror of existence in California. The narrator reflects on her own illusion of immigration. In America, she has no liberty to walk openly on the pavement. She shares her suffocation with her niece. While the move about in open areas, they are humiliated by being called as 'nigger'. The violent attacks of these boys make them nervous. The feeling of alieness grips her consciousness and she becomes impatient to go back home. She reveals her anxiety, 'Home', I whisper desperately, home, home, home.' I want my room in Calcutta; I want the high mahogany bed. I want my childhood again. The horrors of the existence in bi-cultural spaces ruin the sensibility of Indian immigrants.

Jayanti uncle's speech reveals that there are vast cultural differences between the two countries, there is heavily discrimination in employment, there is no social life and there are only low profile jobs available for Indians. He says that America is fantasy, full of colors but one who enters into it finds nothing but blocked spaces. The writer concludes- that everything in America is a dream and no person has succeeded in becoming an American. Here we notice diversified statements in two different stories by the author. In one story she praises America for converting a timid woman into a bold one and in another story she blames America claiming it as a bare land where immigrants can never find a space to fit into. This proves that one who migrates should try to grab the best from both the worlds and overcome their liminalites. In other words, it means to say that one should adjust and try to adopt.

The new culture though it is difficult and not grumble about it. At this stage, we can refer to Jhumpa Lahiri's short stories. She has evolved her own styles in dealing with sensitive issues by changing the mode of narration from past to the present and again reverting it without being nostalgic. Almost all her short stories end on a positive note, with the hope of 'tomorrow' which suggests that with little effort we can discard our cultural liminalities and move towards a society where the traditional and the modern would meet in the inherent goodness, asserting the worth of human life. All the short stories rightly expose the various diasporic elements such as alienation, rootlessness, familial relations, generation gap, identity crises etc. But finally all these protagonists assimilates the humiliation and firmly decide to stay back instead of escaping from the diasporic elements and fulfill their dreams and quest for existentialism. The woman diasporic writers through their protagonists successfully reveal that culture will change any person to follow it, not out of compulsion but by changing the person's psyche to follow it voluntarily. In this way the liminalities can be overcome if the foreign concept of diaspora is assimilated.

Works Cited

1. Albreet, Milton C. "The Relationship of Literature and Society". American Literature of Sociology, LIX No.5, March, 1954. Print.
2. Chitra, Banerjee Divakaruni. *Arranged Marriage*, Black Swan, Great Britain, 1997. Print.
3. Sansaram, Reena. "Immigrans Dilemma and Feminist Sensibilities" in Chitra BanerjeeDivakaruni's Arranged Marriage". Feminism and Recent Indian Literature, Vol.II(ed)R.K.Dhawan, Delhi: Prestige International Publishing House, 2009. Print.

•••

THE THEME OF EXILE AND SUFFERINGS IN AMITAV GHOSH'S *THE GLASS PALACE*

M. Raja Vignesh
Ph.D Scholar,
Saraswathi Narayanan College, Madurai -22

Dr. M.R. Chandran
Associate Professor and Head
Saraswathi Narayanan College (Autonomous), Madurai -22

Introduction

Exile, involuntary or voluntary has been one of the key themes in several epical narratives of classical and medieval literatures. It is predominantly related to the fall of the kingdoms or deposition of kings landing them into exile or captivity that was the focal point in literature of those times. The cause had been either rivalry between siblings, or in-house struggle for power or invasions. In more recent literatures, especially in postcolonial theory or discourse, the term drifting characterizes the drifting sensibility of people banished or dislocated from a physical location to distant lands, there by forming various Diasporas.

Feminism does not particularly talk of equality and rights of a woman rather it is about compassion, respect and understanding from the male counterparts. The prime reason for the dissatisfaction of women in the present society is the superior attitude of men. All these years, women have suffered in silence and feminism talks exactly about that. Authors like Anita Desai, Shashi Deshpande and Kamala

Markandaya have already used various aspects of the male-dominated society as the prime theme in most of their novels.

Research Objectives

This paper examines the problems faced by the Royal family after they were sent in exile to India from Burma after the invasion of the British, the fall of the Konbuang Dynasty in Mandalay, the impact created in the mind of Rajkumar, the protagonist and how the major women characters of Amitav Ghosh get rid of their dependency, needs, breaking the sexuality and take their place as fellow beings freely and equally along with men.

Exile in *the Glass Palace*

The Glass Palace is a historical novel by Amitav Ghosh. The novel is set in Burma, India and Malaya. The novel is a story of three generations and spans a century from the fall of the Konbuang Dynasty in Mandalay through the Second World War, to the modern times. The novel explores a broad range of issues varying from the changing economy of Burma and India to the relevant questions about, what makes a nation and how the society changes along the tide of modernity. One of such issues is exile. In Postcolonial fiction, the theme of 'exile' sets out the damage or loss that the colonizers did to the colonized. This damage is both physical and psychological. The greatest damage done by the colonizers are in the forms of economic breakdown, social disorientation and identity crisis. The characters in this novel, which are in known and unknown exile lose their identity too. The Postcolonial writers have given profound psychological insights into the pain and predicament of the colonized. Exile in any form shatters the whole being of a person.

Exile refers to an enforced or regretted absence or enforced removal from one's country or homeland or home. The condition of exile involves "the idea of a separation and distancing from either a literal homeland or from a cultural and ethnic origin" (Ashcroft). Thus, Exile can have a number of synonymous importations like banishment, removal, dislocation, separation, shift and isolation and so on. Exile is the omnipresent theme in Amitav Ghosh's *The Glass Palace.*It comes as compulsion or destiny to a number of characters. The protagonist Rajkumar Raha is forced to live in an alien environment. Dolly lives in exile as her destiny. Uma is swinging from place to place. King Thibaw of Burma, along with his Royal family and loyalists is deposed and exiled to India. Besides these major characters, some minor ones too have felt the heat of the exile in this novel. The whole devastation has been caused by the then colonial system.

Rajkumar Raha, the protagonist of the novel, *The Glass Palace,* enters the city of Mandalay in exile. He ends up with doing odd jobs for a food stall owner Ma Cho, an Indo-Burmese by origin. He is in Mandalay by reason of his destiny: "it was chance alone that was responsible for Rajkumar's presence in Mandalay" (TGP 14). He is only a boy of eleven when he is orphaned, all his family die of fever. After the loss of his family he leaves his hometown Chittagong and reaches Mandalay. After the abrupt takeover of the Mandalay Fort by the British forces, the entire political and social set up of Burma faces chaos.

The exile of King Thibaw of Burma along with his family has been depicted in a quite pervasive way. This exile is coerced upon the sovereign of Burma which breaks him and humiliates him a lot. The main reason behind the war on Burma was that the British were demanding hold on the precious teak forests of Burma. Rajkumar mocks at this weird reason behind the invasion:" A war over wood? Who's ever heard of such thing?"(TGP 15), thus criticizing the unreasonable demand of the colonizers. As soon as the British Soldiers intrude into the Mandalay Palace of Burma, there is sudden chaos. The Royal Ministers, courtiers, soldiers, servants and common people, all are disintegrated and turn disobedient and shun their loyalty towards their Royal Crown. The author describes the first betrayal thus:

> The two minsters were now competing with one another to keep the Royal Family under guard. They knew the British would be grateful to whoever handed over the Royal Couple; there would be rich rewards. The foreigners were expected to come to Mandalay very soon to take the King and Queen into captivity (TGP 25).

The Royal family is being sent into exile, the British Government wishes them to provide them an escort of attendants and advisors. The matter is to be settled by asking volunteers who would accompany the King and his family. But, no one from among the ministers, servants and attendants come forward to join the Royal entourage. The King remains impassive as he watches his most trusted servants averting their faces. Everyone is reluctant as they are no more bound to the king, dethroned and exiled: "They were neither the King's friends nor his confidants and it was not in their power to lighten the weight of his crown. The burden of Kingship were Thebaw's alone, solitude not the least among them" (TGP 41). However, the people of Mandalay give a tearful valediction to their King and Queen being "heard into exile" (TGP 44). When the Royal entourage reaches the waterfront, the king witnesses a large number of Indians dislocate themselves from Burma. Some people like Rajkumar stay back. Rajkumar with the help of Saya John enters into the timber business and becomes wealthy. His conscience does not prick him. He unknowingly accepts the capitalistic style of living. He loses his identity as Indian to the clutches of Colonialism. But he does not realise it whereas his future wife Dolly leaves the Palace as a servant-maid to the Royal Couple along with the Royal family. Her fate is all because she is an orphan. The girls like Dolly are recruited to look after the little princesses in the Palace and also in the alien land of Ratnagiri.

Suffering in *the Glass Palace*

Amitav Ghosh portrays his women characters sensitively. In fact they are the lead characters in his novels. He presents his female characters neither radical nor stereotypical. *The Glass Palace* is an extraordinary achievement by Amitav Ghosh. An important incident which occurs in the novel sets the tone of the women characters. Rajkumar, an eleven-year old urchin, works as a helper for Ma Cho. Through the creek in wall he views Ma Cho at nights and female anatomy and sex. He also gets his first physical sensation through her but she resists herself from his advances, "Abruptly, she pushed him away, with a yelp of disgust. What am I doing with this boy, the child, this half-wit kalaa? Elbowing him aside, she clambered up her ladder and vanished into her room" (*The Glass Palace* 57). The situation is saved by the strength and sanity of the woman in the novels of Ghosh and women stand as preserver of culture and spiritual essence.

The British force the Burmese King Thibaw and his Queen Supayalat to exile. Dolly a nine-year old girl looking after the younger princess in the palace, grows into an attractive young girl and attains mental and physical maturity. Her choice is Sawant, a local servant. But Uma, her friend persuades her to marry Rajkumar. Dolly is the spirit of endurance and acceptance. Her weakness is her strength. She stands for courage, honour, compassion, and hope. There is the feeling that the traditional emphasis on feminine virtues like obedience and patience are not like subservience and impotence. This distinction is the first category presupposes agency and the second destroys it. Women possessing the first category of qualities are to be treated as persons.

Meenakshi Mukerjee says, "Social conformity has always been more obligatory for a woman than a man, and generally a woman's identity tends to be defined by herself as well as by others, in terms of relationship with men -- as a daughter, as a wife, and as a mother"(*Image of Woman in Indian Literature* 98). Dolly shows that a woman can fulfil herself in a loving and harmonious relationship with others.

Uma Dey, the wife of the Collector, is very attractive and charming, and of the good friend of Dolly. She is instrumental in the marriage of Dolly with Rajkumar. She began to sob, covering her face with her hands. He had no use for the wifely virtues which she could offere him. Cambridge had taught him to want more; to make sure that nothing was held in abeyance; to bargain for a woman's soul with the coin of kindness and patience"(153). If a man treats his wife as if only he could know what is best for, then it is considered as external constraint and power. She longs for companionship based on understanding and love and for autonomy for self. She finds it difficult to cope with this atmosphere of constrained enchantment. The women in the novel try to get different levels of liberation.

Conclusion:

The author depicts numerous instances of exile that intensify the overall impact of colonialization on the masses of colonies. The novel dissects the new world created under the authority of the Empire which comprises a strange mélange of aliens and exiles: Indians in Burma, Burmese in India and Malaysia, Malaccans in Burma and India, British in Burma and Indians in America. The Burmese are presented entirely as victims of colonial politicking. *The Glass Palace* depicts how unjustified and inhumane were the British in pushing indigenous people to displacement, captivity, loot, exile and capitalistic exploitation. The novel brings to the fore the question of the displaced, implicitly indicting the colonizers for dislodging the innocent natives from their homeland.

Ghosh's fiction portrays woman as a life-giver, sustainer and continuer of the race. The image of perfect but very human beauty lies in the character of Dolly. In continuity of the tradition developed by Tagore, Narayan, Saghal, Ghosh develops women who are strong, can express themselves, do things and live independently. They practise ideas which they as individuals value. In Uma Dey, we find a fusion of Psychological and Sociological traumata. It is a continuous discussion of values and relationships.

Works Cited

1. Ashcroft, Bill, Gareth Griffiths and et.al., *Key Concepts in Postcolonial Studies.* London and New York: Routledge, 1998. Print.
2. Bhat, Yashoda & Yamuna Raja Rao.(eds.).*The Image of Woman in Indian Literature.* New Delhi: B.R.Publishing Corporation, 1993, Print.
3. Ghosh, Amitav. *THE GLASS PALACE.* Noida: Harper Collins Publishers, 2016, Print.
4. Meenakshi Mukerjee

CROSSING FRONTIERS: CELEBRATIONS OF LIFE

R. Rohini
Assistant Professor of English
Mannar Thirumalai Naicker College (Self Financing Wing) Madurai

Dr. M. R. Chandran
Associate Professor of English, S.N. College, Madurai

Abstract

Mangoes on the Maple Tree is a debut novel of Uma Parameswaran, which popularised the novelist in diasporic literature to great heights leading her to the most debated writer in the canon of Indo-Canadian Literature. Her novel focuses on alienation, displacement, nostalgia and loss of identity.

The novel Mangoes on the Maple Tree delves forcefully into the lives of an Indo-Canadian family.The characters portrayed undergo traumatic experiences as they struggle to fit into the new environment. They are conscious of their national identity in everything they do.

Keywords: *Diaspora, Alienation, Adoption, Assimilation.*

Analysis:

The paper is an attempt to analyse the diasporic sensibilities as depicted in the novel *The Mangoes on the Maple Tree* through the prominent characters Jayant and Jyoti.

Uma Parameswaran being a much debated and a noted diasporic writer underscores the psyche of the immigrants. Parameswaran skillfully delineates the lives of the two different families-Bhaves and their cousins the Moghes amidst the background of the floods in Winnipeg,Manitoba in the year 1997.The study demands a close analysis of the two characters namely Jayant and Jyoti from the Bhave family.The novel at the outset appears to be different and in contrast to other novels like *Anita and Me* by Meera Sayal and *The Namesake* by Jhumpa Lahiri.It also offers a different dimension of the diasporic situation.

The Bhave family now migrates to Winnipeg dishing out their luxurious life.They were always served and helped by their servants..To add to it Sharad, the father of the two children Jayanth and Jyoti was a nuclear scientist. The children were deprived of their elite lifestyle as they lived in India. Initially they find it too hard to sustain themselves in a new environment. To them, life in Canada is no bed of roses. Thatthe readers can clearly comprehend the concept of domestic helps is not a possibility at all. But the question of doubt arises here.Is it difficult for an individual to do the domestic work for one's own family? Adapting to one's situation, the way life offers is the only solution. The researcher is of the opinion that this should not be a great hindrance for the diasporans to live their life.The family unit is all that matters.However,it is possible for them to tide over.

The narrative begins with Jayant's plan for a road trip with his friends. The Bhaves are unpleasant about his going because they always nurture the archetypal values of the diasporans. They always believe in being and spending time with their respective families,and are strongly rooted in their tradition. Robin Cohen in his *Diaspora and the Nation:State from Victims to Challengers* asserts this "as a strong ethnic group consciousness" (Cohen 55).

Jyoti and Krish,before Jayant would embark on his Journey emphasises with much sentiments that they would miss him and his absence would be felt intensely. "I am going to miss you Bhau" writes Uma Parameswaran.She further continues in the novel *Mangoes on the Maple Tree,*

> He stopped himself short, realizing he had used a forbidden word. Back in Pune, he and all their cousins his age had called older brothers and cousins Bhau as was the custom, but Jayant has shed his Indianisms fast and he had dinned it out of others with his derisive taunts...And if you must go for all these crappy familiarities,say Auntie Vee, not Vee Auntie for chrissake(6).

The above quote confirms Jayant's assimilation and adoption of Canadian culture and speech. He fits as a fiddle in the Canadian climate.

The dispute between Jayant and his sister Jyoti about being foreigners or strangers in an alien soil is transparent as he chides his younger brother, not to address him as 'Bhau'.The episode showcases how Jayant is determined to give up his indianess as he tries to adapt in another country, Canada,a land of his family's choice.

However Jyoti his sister, recalls their way of living in India, and that their father, by now would have become the director of Indian Institute of Technology, as he was a scientist at the time of leaving India for good. Whereas, life is not full bed of roses now for, their father has to mow his own lawn by himself, rot here pursuing a menial profession as a real estate broker. This was not the case in their hometown because he had hired attendants and servants to help him. This can never happen in Canada, for the natives live in the ideology of no maids. All those who choose to migrate to such countries know that they have to do their own chores and when an individual comes to terms with such living there is nothing to worry about. The solution lies in adopting the lifestyle of the country. To be precise when in Rome do as Romans do.

The concept of luxurious living as in India, in countries like Canada it is unthinkable. Jyotiis consciousof wide differences between the two countries.Her feeling of otherness wells up beyond measure. It surfaces at all levels.It is true that one's place of origin and one's culture and tradition play a vital role in the determination of one's identity but individuals need to be wise in the decision making.Once a decision is made and executed, there is no reason to go back and ruminate on it; otherwise, it would eventually bring catastrophe.

The oscillation is evident in the minds of the characters afore mentioned. Both of them feel suffocated and damned as immigrants.Jayant as an immigrant reminiscence his past way of life in India and Jyoti is conscious of being the "other". The infinitesimal details of the history of his family which he bequeathed through his bed time stories haunt him.Both of them are in absolute state of in - betwenness.But whatever may be their defences one finds, Jayant insisting on not to call anyone by 'Bhau' is evident of his shedding of the Indian way of addressing. It is apparent that he is ofcourse trying to adapt and adopt Canadian way of speaking and living.

Jyoti's relationship with Pierre and her loadstone towards Sridhar are symbolic of two different cultures-two diverging influences on her identity formation. And the sense of attraction towards both of them represents her state of in-betweenness.Thus she suffers emotionally. But as the novel moves on,one understands that she does not want to continue her relationship with Pierre for her own reasons.If this is what she decides where is the question of losing one's identity? When one chooses to do what she wills, she is obviously independent.

• • •

Stuart Hall in his work *Cultural Identity and Diaspora* exemplifies:

Far from being externally fixed in some essentialised past, they are subject to the continuous 'play' of history, culture and power... identifies are the names we give to the different ways we are positioned by, and position ourselves within, the narrative of the past. (394)

Thus, the identities one takes depends on oneself. It is important to mention that the writer of the novel taken for analysis is neither an Indian nor a Canadian but an Indo-Canadian. Does she not have an identity of her own?

The argument is based on the two prominent Uma Parameswaran's characters taken for the study.The researcher strongly argues that when one chooses to leave his or her own country to live in an another country,for greener pastures or for reasons of their own, where is the question of suffering? Why does one look out for mangoes on a maple tree? One should perceive a maple tree with characteristics of its own and enjoy maple jam or maple syrup instead of looking out for mangoes.The mind needs to be trained.One can make a hell out of heaven and a heaven out of hell.The mind and one's life is inter dependent.

Uma Parameswaran dexterously portrays the diasporic sensiblities by focusing on alienation,immigrant experiences, state of in-betweeness,loss of identity,assimilation and many more through her finest debut novel *Mangoes on the Maple Tree.* As an Indo-Canadian writer she plunges into the finest of feelings of the Indians settled in Canada.She leaves her readers free to analyse and arrive at a solution feasible for themselves.Being an ardent admirer of the writer,the researcher after having made a thorough study, feels that there is no point in always crying about the alien land being different and strange. It can never be ones mother country for sure but one should embrace the land, adopt and adaptto the land, where one chooses voluntarily to live. This should be the mantra for healthy and holistic communal living, for life is a celebration and crossing frontiers says it all.

Works Cited

1. Cohen, Robin. *Dispora and Nation – State: from Victims to Challangers*. Volume 72, No. 3, JSTOR, July 1996. Print.
2. Parameswaran, Uma. *Mangoes on the Maple Tree*. New York: iUniverse Inc, 2006. Print.
3. Mirzoeff, Nicholas Ed. *Dispora and Virtual Culture : Representing African and Jews*. Hall, Stuart. "Cultural Identity and Dispora." UK: Routledge, 1999. Print.

FEMININE CONSCIOUSNESS IN GITHA HARIHARAN'S THE THOUSAND FACES OF NIGHT

Dr. M.R. Chandran
Associate Professor
Centre for Research in English,
Saraswathi Narayanan College, Madurai

Githa Hariharan is a promising voice in the spectrum of women writers who champion the cause of women rights in full throat. Her literature is qualified to be an act, not a mere writing. It is dictated by the commitment of creating a new history for women who have been denied history for long. She is aggressively committed to overthrow all the male-conceived social practices which consider women as possessions, not persons, an appendix to male life. Woman's life from womb to tomb is punctured with painful stories scripted by patriarchy.

Githa Hariharan finds misogyny as the root cause of the global distress, burial of which will pave way for the social harmony to make a heaven of life. Her works, rather researches on gender injustice command reverential attention for their authenticity, gravity and magnitude of giving insightful understanding of the social detrimental patriarchy. Digesting the ideas of Simon de Beauvoir and Virginia Wolf, Hariharan's stories, empathetically longing for gender equality explore and document the oppressed lives of woman. She infuses her own personal emotions and couched experience from real life into her characters to make them her strong and bold mouthpieces and the epitome of righteousness and bravery. Hariharan in her personal life, has fought for her rights as a mother and she questioned the subjectivity of the Hindu Minority and Guardianship Act. She has won the legal battle of claiming the right to name the child after the mother who is also the natural guardian of the child.

Githa Hariharan documents her own understanding of the concept of patriarchy that it is the enforced quintessence which legitimizes the violence of men and sanctifies the sexual dominance of men over women where they are licensed to exploit them. She seriously enquires about the inferior roles given to women in the male-critic novels in sync with Simon de Beauvoir and poor treatment of women in real life and analyses their behavioural patterns of tackling the overhanded operation of patriarchy. She excels in her own way of interpreting stereotypical ethos of the society to make the audience convinced of the definite agenda of her writings. She delves deep into the people of the Indian society to surface the cruel nature of patriarchy in its complete spirit which bulldozes the rights of women unempathetically. She considers herself as an 'engaged citizen' to experiment the smothered dark history of womanhood in the clutches of Satanic patriarchy.

In her novels Hariharan questions subjective interpretation of myth of patriarchy to its favour and enlightens an objective understanding of myth which advocates liberty, equality and dignity of humanity. Hariharan's novels are realistic that they characterize both the weak and strong women though latter is attached more emphasized. The weak and submissive characters like Mayamma, Sita, Mangla, Laxmi and Bala who make passive submission to the dominance of men and the revolutionary characters like Devi, Parvatiamma, Shahrzad, Dwnyazad, Meena, Mala, Sara and Yasmin who do not encourage any opportunity for men to stain their lives.

Githa Hariharan's *The Thousand Faces of Night* provides a comfortable site to understand deeply the evolution in the behavioural spirit of women of three generations. The novel documents the underground lives of Indian women. It explores the simplicity and exposure of women to the bludgeoned male scripted subordinate roles in their daily lives. Deepak Kumar Singh comments on this:

> The novel is about the lives of women, their strategies of survival in this normative and cruel world of patriarchy. It also concerns itself with the art of storytelling in a measured way. In broader and more general terms, it may be placed in the category of women's writing about women's lives, especially inner lives which unfold a hitherto unopened and vast panorama of female psyche and female experience.

The weakest of all the women character is Mayamma who is created as a warning to the women folk from being the prey to the patriarchal unjust obligations and to create a sense of awareness and arouse the spirit of feminism among the women, particularly tradition wedded women exposing them to the untold tortures that Mayamma has been inflicted upon. She has been trained to be traditional women to dance to the tune of men and honour the patriarchal dictations. She was married off at the tender age of twelve in her prime innocent to make a hell of married enslaved life where she is deprived of her due space in the domestic climate and of any due rights. The writer criticizes such woman who miserably fail to discover their potential to revolt to claim their rights but stay silent to be tied as puppets to the fingers of men and act to the pull of the strings.

The character Sita of second generation is also dictated by patriarchal norms forebearing the pains of inequality and discrimination. She is thrown to an aggressive domestic climate where her individuality, freedom, dream, aspiration, desires become casualty. Her passion for playing Veena to make it her career is severely suppressed. Though Sita's husband is not a hardcore patriarchy practitioner like Mayamma's husband, he denies his wife's rightful privileges pushing her to sickening life. These unjust restriction imprison her to a suffocated life of ineffectual angel. Ruby Davaseeli states "Sita has set a role model in her own devotion to her husband and family. In the chain of actions and reactions, one can see how the family first distorts and represses women's desire and then co-opts or browbeats them into submission to its structure (53). Inevitably Sita's daughter Devi also is cast the same spells of life of her mother. She shows the plight of wife who has to be dependent on her husband who is insensitive to her emotions, "I am a wooden puppet in his hands. I stand by him, a silent wife, my wet sari clinging to me like a parasite" (Thousand Nights 83). However Devi's education abroad comes to her rescue to make realize her duty to honour the rights of her life. She braves her heart to break the shackles of the patriarchy. She makes her life untouched by the influences of neither the myths and stories nor the behaviour of her husband and father-in-law. She refuses to be a common traditional woman pawning her independent life to patriarchal demands. She questions her husband encroaching uopon her natural rights and confronts her husband whenever and wherever he tries to maltreat her whipping out grave discrimination and inequality. She tries to script a new and constructive story of womanhood and preaches men to understand and admit it to achieve social harmony. Devi, as typical mouth piece of Githa Hariharan interprets the myths and the stories in feministic fashion justifying the mythological figure Gangaa in the Mahabharatha leaving her husband who violated the marriage promises and vows. She is convinced with her decision of leaving her husband inspired by Gangaa's determination as Mahesh character, her husband does not revere the wholly nature of the marriage and not care for the bond of pious love and promises of marriage where the husband and wife are the spiritual partners.

The characters in *The Thousands Faces of Night* are fried down with augmented and repetitive discrimination and injustice of the patriarchy which awakens the feminism in them. Devi escaping from doll's house finds bliss in her new world where she discovers great meaning of her life. The mother and daughter lastly get united making themselves freed from the prison life of harassment and discrimination experiencing emotionally psychologically socially mentally domestically healthy environment which stands in contrast to the old one. Githa Hariharan wilfully effects such a juxtaposition of themes to drive home the fact that only those who dare to fight win the fight and get to cherish such blissfull moments of life.

Woman should have equality with men in every sphere of life, be it social, economic, political or religious. Natural strong nature of women is made corroded with reproaching codes of patriarchy that leads to lethal devaluation of women and degeneration of their self-identity.

One is given to understand how the education and reconstruction of mythology help women in getting awareness of the oppression and about the tools to use against it. Women should empower themselves fighting the social virus misogyny with renewed determination and tenacity to achieve gender disparity-free society.

Works Cited

1. Davaseeli, Ruby. *Women and Family in Recent Indian Feminist Fiction in English.*
2. Dissertation. Pondicherry University, 2011. Web.2 July 2015.
3. Hariharan, Githa. *The Thousand Faces of Night.* New Delhi:Penguin Books, 1992. Print
4. Singh, Deepak Kumar. *Marginal Voices of the Novels of Githa Hariharan.* Jaipur.
5. Y King Books, 2015. Print

THE CONCEPT OF HOME IN INDIAN DIASPORIC LITERATURE

Dr. T. Senthamarai
Associate Professor, Department of English
VELS Institute of Science, Technology and Advanced Studies, Chennai

The concept of 'home' in Diaspora literature is as complex as the human mind which is intertwined with web of memories. It is multi-layered and produces multiple meanings of the term 'home'. This article tries to study what exactly the term means in Indian Diaspora writings and proves the point that the home is nowhere but in the mind of the individual who carry memories of home which is always fluid. The concept of home has been overstated in the writings of Diaspora. While it is important to keep in mind that the physical home- house has its own connections, the metaphysical house- home has a higher level of connotations.

Most Indian diasporic literature deals with one focal point; searching the lost home which eventually end up a myth. The best example that expresses the state of Diaspora is to quote Jumpa Lahiri's 'The Third and Final Continent'. In which she describes,

> "While the astronauts, heroes forever, spent mere hours on the moon, I have remained in this new world for nearly thirty years. I know that my achievement is quite ordinary. I am not the only man to seek his fortune far away from home, and certainly I am not the first. Still there are times I am bewildered by each mile I have travelled, each meal I have eaten, each person I have known, each room in which I have slept. As

ordinary as it all appears, there are times when it is beyond my imagination.

The omniscient narrator in Jumpa Lahiri: The Third and Final Continent' (1999:198)

The term 'diaspora' often trigger the context of home in the readers mind. As Brubaker (2005:2) views that the concept of diaspora literature has been 'firmly rooted in a conceptual "homeland"'. It is undeniable that when people migrate from one place to another, one country to another, as in the case of diaspora writings, they are compelled to bring their memories back with them. The compelling memories of home is more psychological than physical. The role of a mind in formation of memories is inexplicable to ordinary human beings who are prone to be sentimental. They allow memories to possess their lives than the newly taken up robe; the role in the new setting. That said, it is impossible for anyone to distance oneself from memory. Hence, the mind plays an inescapable part in diaspora literature.

Claire Alexander debates, 'the significance and performance of memory in transnational or diasporic communities and spaces has remained comparatively unexplored'. The nature of homeland memories are different but focuses more on ethnic, family attachments, celebrations, and events, both painful and pleasant. William Safran supports this view in his observation that; "---they continue to relate personally or vicariously, to the homeland in a way or another, and their ethnic-communal consciousness and solidarity are importantly defined by the existence of such a relationship." (Safran, 1991:23)

While giving life to memories, we allow the past to become present thereby gaining new attention and new life. Shared memories of the past is quintessential in shaping up the present. Diasporic memory is formed unwillingly and are quotidian memories of home. After becoming a diaspora, one is pushed to the extent of recalling everyday events, incidents, life of the past and collective memory is at most at use. There is a constant struggle between two homes: home of the past and home of the present. While portraying the struggle and survival of a home, Jumpa Lahiri says, "The difference was so extreme that he could not accommodate the two places together in mind…Both places were so close to sea level, with estuaries where fresh and salt water combined…" (2013:34). Lahiri goes on to say,

> Sailing even slightly east reminded Subhash of how far he was from his family …. He felt doubly alone. Unable to fathom his future, severed from his past (….) It was the distance between America and India; the distance that how separated him from his family…. He didn't belong, but perhaps it didn't matter. He wanted to tell her that he had been waiting all his life to find Rhode Island. That it was here, in this minute but majestic corner of the world, that he could breathe (Lahiri 2013: 62-65)

Search for home is a subconscious act of mind which tries to relate home to identity and existence. Besides being an act of the intellect, the search for home is an active engagement of the self with oneself. The self involves in constant conversation; a conversation with a metahome. As Salman Rushdie observers; "--- one physical alienation from India at almost inevitably means that we will not be capable of redeeming precisely the thing that was lost, that will, in short, create fictions not actual cities or villages, but invisible ones, imaginary homelands, Indians of mind."(Rushdie, 1991:10)

Nevertheless, the pertinent question remains, what is home? And where is it?

The choice, either deliberate or otherwise, that most of the diasporic community makes in settling down in another country results in finding a new home at the cost of the old one. However, the memories of the old home keeps haunting and prevents from embracing the new. The mind is pushed to inbetweenness creating a pendulum which oscillates. The oscillation is between the past and present, here and there. Vijay Agnew views, "... the individual living in the diaspora experiences a dynamic tension everyday between living 'here' and remembering 'there', between memories of places of origin and between the metaphorical and physical home" (2005:4).

For instance, the main characters of Jumpa Lahiri have strong value systems of the homeland. They are equally strong in both holding on to the systems of the homeland as well the desire to cling on to the present home. As much as they find pleasure in recalling the memories of the past, they are self-assertive venturing into the present and take pride in it. Though the oscillation does not give a sense of completion, a fulfilled life in one home, it certainly gives them the feeling of living double lives with double homes.

While living in two places, the characters live in a state of fluidity, a state of being transferred and hence translated. This can be best understood from Rushdie's Imaginary Homeland. He views, "Having been across the world, we are translated men. It is normally supposed that something always gets lost in translation." In order to compensate the lost and missed self, the human mind tries to manipulate with memories of the events of the same. By reminiscing the past, the present tries to convince oneself whereby creating an equilibrium though it is hard to do.

Not only the characters search and long for their permanent home, the writers of diaspora find themselves in limbo. Jhumpa Laheri's sense of home is expressed when she views that no country is her home: "No country is my motherland. I always find myself in exile whichever country I travelled to, that is why I was tempted to write on something about this that is living their lives in exile". (Nityanandam, 2005). The eternal quest of lost home affects the writers of all generations. V.S. Naipaul has expressed the inability of finding a home in The House for Mr.Biswas, a metaphorical house. "The Mimic Man" of V.S.Naipaul is another instance where the protagonist, a student, struggles in London.

Ian Chambers views, "migrancy is a movement in which neither the points of departure nor arrival is certain" and it is a "constant mutation…always in transit with no promise of homecoming" (1994:5). The feeling of transit and always on the move results in frustration of not having a permanent home. The sense of belonging to a place, a home, becomes irresistible as it creates close link to one's identity. Chambers goes on to say, "An incomplete journey, no fixed identity or final destination" (Chambers, 1994:25).

Nonetheless, it is evident that one home has to be fluid while other can be solid. It is left to the individual to choose. Syrian American Writer and poet Mohja Kahf says the difficulty in choosing the one. She express in her poem, "The Passing There",

Impossible for us
to choose one over the other,
and the passing there
makes all the difference, (2006)

Passing is a process, sometimes turns to be a progress. In the process of passing through, we, the human beings are destined to encounter many things; experiences and lessons; a collective memory. Ahmed views, "a process of becoming estranged from that which was inhabited at home". (1999:343).

When the acculturalization takes place, the memories are diluted and acceptance takes place through a process of realization. The place they used to call home remains a place of memory, a mental space.

The search for home or accepting the new home becomes a choice, a wise choice to make. The wiser the choice the better and the brighter the life will be in the new home. Homelessness, in-betweenness can be overcome by wilful and conscious effort. Majaj claims, "rather, what is needed is the ability to move with fluidity between worlds" (Majaj, 2008:10). The reconciliation and coming to terms with reality opens up new perspectives and free oneself from the clutches of the past. Though the smell, sounds, feelings, celebrations, friends, school, the mango tree….brings nostalgic feeling, the mission of migration will be fulfilled only when the reality is accepted.

Avtar Brah and Uma Parmesvaran urge that embracing and accepting the new norm / home is the wise thing to do by crossing the psychic border more than the geographical border and Uma Paramesvaran asserts that "Both exile and home is here, within the new homeland."(Parmeswaran, 2003:107). That said, the real and original memories of home of the past doesn't have to be ignored rather it can be carried in the heart pleasantly. As Jarrar says, "Our people carry the homeland in their souls" and continues to say, "you can go wherever you want, but you'll always have it in your heart (Jarrar, 2008:9). As the Turkish writer Elif Shafak, in her Ted Talks, asserts, the home is portable, a symbol of freedom.

Work Cited

1. Agnew, Vijay. "Introduction." In Diaspora, Memory and Identity: A Search for Home, ed. VijayAgnew (Toronto: University of Toronto Press, 2005), 3-17.

2. Ahmed, S. "Home and Away: Narratives of Migration and Estrangement". International Journal of Cultural Studies, 2.3, (1999):329-347.
3. Chambers, I. Migrancy, Culture, Identity. Routledge, New York, 1994.
4. Jarrar, R. A Map of Home, Other Press, New York, 2008.
5. Majaj, L.S. "Arab - American Literature: Origins and Developments", American Studies Journal 52, np. Retrieved Mar.20, 2020, http://www.asjurnal.org/archive/52/150.html.
6. Nityanandam, Indira. "Jhumpa Laheri: The Tale of the Diaspora". New Delhi, Creative Books, 2005.
7. Parmeswaran, Uma. "Home is where your feet are, and may your heart be there too". Writers of the Indian Diaspora. Ed. Jasbir Jain. New Delhi: Rawat Publications, 2003. 107. Print.
8. Rushdie, Salman. "Imaginary Homelands: Essays and Criticism". London, Grants Books, 1994.
9. Safran, W. "Diasporas in modern societies: myths of homeland and return", Diaspora: A Journal of Transnational Studies, 1 (1), 83 -99, doi:10.1353/dsp.1991.0004.